PRAISE FOR *BREAKING*

'This book is a timely, lively and lucid account
increasing triumphs – of women in sport, as the
tilted in favour of men ... a vital contribution to the debate on women in sport.'
*The Weekend Australian*

'Pippos' discussion of the ingrained bias against women in sport is framed within
an unabashed, feminist context and drawn from her own considerable experience
as one of the few female sports journalists ... In her innervating and timely book
Angela Pippos has supplied some great ammunition for the cause
of girls and women in sport.'
*The Sydney Morning Herald*

'A compelling overview of women in sport breaking through the "grass ceiling".
Pippos is well placed to document the transformation for women's sports from
no media coverage to front page news. Verdict: Inspiring.'
*The Sunday Territorian*

'Angela Pippos is the sporting scribe of our times. She takes a hammer – no, a
sledgehammer, but a fun, searing and occasionally funny one – to the sexism that is
pervasive in sport, be it in our attitudes, media, codes or our funding or policies.'
Natasha Stott Despoja AM, Chair of Our Watch

'A truly marvellous book ... like having a fabulously extended, engaging deep
and meaningful conversation with Angela. [She] speaks on behalf of all those
girls and women who know that playing sport makes them feel
powerful and strong and free.'
Dr Clare Wright, best-selling author of *Beyond the Ladies Lounge: Australia's
Female Publicans* and *The Forgotten Rebels of Eureka*

'A truly eye-opening and timely book, a superbly written call to arms for
equality ... The persuasive prose and impassioned tone is sure to challenge and
change more than a few viewpoints, and ultimately will go a long way towards
helping everyone get on the same playing field.'
*Right Now*

**AFFIRM**press

Angela Pippos is a journalist, writer, television and radio presenter, film producer and public speaker based in Melbourne.

ANGELA PIPPOS

# BREAKING

# THE

# MOULD

**Affirm press**

Published by Affirm Press in 2017
28 Thistlethwaite Street, South Melbourne, VIC 3205.
www.affirmpress.com.au

10 9 8 7 6 5 4 3

National Library of Australia Cataloguing-in-Publication entry available
for this title.
Title: Breaking the Mould / Angela Pippos, author.
ISBN: 9781925344585 (paperback)

Cover design by Josh Durham, Design by Committee
Typeset in 11.25/17 Sabon by J&M Typesetting
Proudly printed in Australia by Griffin Press

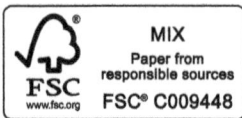

*To Simon, for his love and counsel.*

# CONTENTS

# INTRODUCTION

My partner and I once played a game of golf with his childhood friend from Utah. It is something I will never forget.

Mister Utah was knee-deep in thick, wild grass when I saw him throw his golf ball. His eyes met mine and widened in horror just as the white ball left his hand. It sailed over my head before plopping onto the green below. If I'd been down by the flag, I would have shouted, 'Great shot!' But I was ten metres away, watching him execute the perfect lob – without the use of his pitching wedge.

Sometimes, during moments of great awkwardness, it's best not to say anything, and that was the approach he took; his red face and the slackness of his jaw said it all. So, I followed his lead, and in the excruciatingly silent stand-off we came to a tacit understanding: we both pretended that it hadn't happened.

The fact that the loser had to buy lunch upped the ante of Mister Utah's crime in my mind and stopped me from telling my partner until later that day that his friend had cheated.

'You're joking,' my partner said.

'No.'

'Really?'

'Really. It was horrible – for both of us. The look on his face.'

'He *cheated*?'

'Well, I don't remember Tiger Woods ever throwing his ball out of the rough.'

'I can't believe it, he's a fucking Mormon – he doesn't even drink!'

And off he went …

The ferocity of my partner's disapproval really stuck with me. Over the years, I've retold this story many times, and the reaction, especially from golfers, is always the same – one of complete and utter indignation.

No one ever cheats at golf. Ever. Hardly anyone admits to cheating at sport, but with golf there's an almost messianic zeal when the topic of fair play comes up. Setting a golf cart on fire and driving it into the clubhouse dressed as a member of the Third Reich is more acceptable than giving your ball a nudge forward onto a better lie.

When I've spoken with these same dedicated golfers about the fact that women are excluded from becoming members of the prestigious Muirfield Golf Club in Scotland, their reactions have been quite enlightening (and have helped motivate me to write this book). They always waffle on about tradition but concede that, in this day and age, those rules are a little out of step, a little outdated, a little unfair. The sense of moral outrage shown towards cheating just isn't there. To me this seems like a hugely understated reaction – like sawing your arm off with a chainsaw and going, 'Oops!'

And this problem isn't unique to golf. As a woman working in the sports media for the past twenty years, I've always felt gutted by the 'shrug of the shoulders' response that I get whenever any discussion about gender equality in sport comes up. Talking about fairness and actually being fair are two very different things.

We Australians certainly like to talk about fairness. It's a national pastime, embedded into the DNA of our vernacular: 'a fairer Australia', 'the land of the fair go', 'a fair crack of the whip', 'fair dinkum', 'fair enough', 'a fair suck of the sav' – even our former prime minister Kevin Rudd got in on the act with his mantra-like usage of 'a fair shake of the sauce bottle'.

Sport is our national obsession, and its foundations are built on the idea of fair play. Everyone who takes part is meant to have a sporting chance at victory. Among men, sport has long been considered a place where class and race are irrelevant. Sport is the place where everyone gets a fair go (in theory, anyway). Once you cross over the line, things like your skin colour, your background and your accent don't hold sway like they do in the nine-to-five world. Cross over the line and you are only as good as your abilities. Sport is a wonderful way for people from diverse backgrounds to enter the public arena, to speak for their communities and feel welcomed. It can be a pathway to success for men from disadvantaged backgrounds as much as for the wealthy. Sport can unify, and it can equalise.

When we feel that fairness is being taken away from us, we cry foul: a goal awarded when it was touched on the line, a goal awarded when a player was offside, a catch that didn't carry to third slip, a holding-the-ball decision when the player had no chance of getting rid of it. Fair go, umpire.

When it comes to fairness, sport talks a hell of a good game – the trouble is, it only talks for half of the population. There's a problem with the way Australians (and our overseas competitors) tend to think about and treat women's sport, and it affects everybody.

Everyone should be treated equally. It's not fair to deny girls and women the chance to test their bodies to the limit. It's not fair that teenage girls drop out of sport because female role models are invisible and 'you can't be what you can't see'. It's not fair that elite sportswomen are undervalued and underpaid. It's not fair that women athletes don't have clear pathways in sport and access to the best facilities. It's not fair that women and girls have to use that solitary toilet cubicle plonked at the end of a stretch of urinals. It's not fair, and it's harmful, to peddle the myth that a woman's body is valuable only when she's showing it off, not when she's performing remarkable sporting feats – and it's not fair that sponsorship dollars are linked to how little an athlete wears in a photo shoot. It's not fair when women athletes are ignored by the media. And it's not fair that women are underrepresented in positions of power, despite all evidence showing that gender-diverse boards are good for business.

This is the uneven playing field of Australian sport. It's not neatly confined to the football codes, or cricket, or horseracing, or golf – or anything else, for that matter. The attitude that sport is 'men's business' is deeply rooted in all sports where we all participate: it's as much a part of sport as running, sweating and moaning about the umpire.

*

When I set about writing this book in early 2015, I was filled with a sense of dread – I wanted to discuss the topic of equality, but after my two decades of covering sport, not much had changed for women, and I was finding it hard to feel positive about the future.

Little did I know that as the year unfolded I would be scrambling to keep up with developments and missing deadlines while pleading my case to my publisher for more time. But all the while I was writing, I knew something very special was unfolding. I wrote not with foreboding but with joy – and as any writer will tell you, you get a hell of a lot more done when you don't feel crushed by the weight of it all. The only headshaking that I was doing was at the speed of it all: the speed at which change was taking place, and the speed at which the conversation was changing. Everyone in Australia was finding it impossible to ignore women in sport.

2015 was a breakout year on all fronts for our sportswomen.

Don't think for a minute that everything is perfect, but something wonderful is happening. A turning point has been reached – and I didn't think I'd be writing those words when I had the idea and signed on for this book. At last, meaningful progress is being made. Attitudes that have kept women marginalised in sport are disappearing, clearing the way for a new era of respect and recognition – and with it more media coverage, sponsorship and better pay deals for women athletes.

There's still a long way to go, but women in sport are fighting back and finally breaking the mould.

PART ONE

# The Problem

# 1

# FOR THE LOVE OF SPORT

I am Catwoman.

I'm crouched and ready to pounce. I'm a mass of potential energy waiting to convert, to explode, to launch myself, catlike, left or right. My hands are cupped in anticipation, and my elbows angle towards my tummy while I bounce lightly on my toes, dancing side to side on closely cropped grass and waiting for my brain to pull the trigger, like it's done a thousand times before – don't think, just let the training, instinct and skill take over.

I am nine years old, and this is serious business.

As a child, Sir Donald Bradman developed a solitary game where he would repeatedly hit a golf ball with a cricket stump against the curved brick base of the family water tank in Bowral. He would construct Test matches in his head, pitting himself against the unpredictable balls 'delivered' by the tank stand.

My younger brother, Chris, and I have our own version – instead of a water tank, we use the stem of the rotary clothesline.

Perfect for slips catching practice; perfect to test ourselves against the unpredictable rebound of ball off pole. We spend every available moment refining our skills, and this game, more than any other, demonstrates our dedication.

I'm wearing a shiny tracksuit (I have a collection, one for every day of the week), and I'm squatting on a perfectly manicured lawn a few feet away from the clothesline. The ball hits the metal pole at speed and rebounds at right angles, flying past my left side. I react quickly – of course I do, I'm Catwoman! – shifting my weight and diving after it, arm outstretched.

*Thump.* The beautiful, clean noise of the tennis ball hitting and sticking into my palm.

I lie on the ground, my hand squeezing the yellow, slightly furry ball as I hold it aloft. '*Hoooooooooooowzat!!!*' I spring to my feet, toss the ball high into the sky and finish the routine with a soccer-inspired lap of the lawn, high-fiving the bottlebrush on the way through, giddy on the simple pleasure of catching a tennis ball – albeit, one that had no right to be caught.

'You could play for Australia,' says my brother.

'I know.'

I show him the grass burn on my knuckles. My war wound. My reminder. To both him and me. Of my greatness.

It's been a long session. Mum calls us in for dinner, but we know that she'll call us twice more, so we don't move until her third and final call to come inside and wash our hands. We cross the lawn and dissect our session. There's no argument about my catch – it's definitely going on our scribbled tally of 'classic catches' on the fridge door.

\*

I credit those early years for my sharp reflexes today. I can catch just about anything that suddenly drops or projectiles around the house. As the mother of a toddler, this skill can't be underestimated. Not a day goes by without something toppling off the table or rocketing towards me at speed: crayons, mini-bocconcini, mushrooms, toy cars, grapes. One of the earliest sentences my son, Francis, uttered was, 'Good catch, Mum.' I'd just caught an airborne cherry tomato that he'd launched at my head. After I registered what he said, I followed up with a victory lap of the kitchen. Proud of him – and the catch.

Whenever I see a Hills hoist, I'm instantly transported back to that other world of grass stains and glory. My head fills with a strange mix of nostalgia and a hard-to-pinpoint tinge of sadness. In the kick-to-kick games that we played with all the neighbourhood kids, there was never a big deal made about who could or couldn't play. Other girls played too – some were good, some not so – but that didn't matter. Our games were always played in a tough, but fair and inclusive, spirit. Children are good at that.

Sport was our religion, so we lived for Saturdays, when school and club matches took place. A holy day for us, a day of ritual. Four hours before designated kick-off, Chris would clomp around the house in his polished footy boots, ball under his arm. I'd be dressed at breakfast in my green-and-gold netball uniform. I was convinced (and had managed to convince my brother) that this gaudy combination was a portent of greater things to come. I slept with a copy of Joyce Brown's *Netball the Australian Way* under my pillow, hoping it would stimulate dreams of netball greatness that would rub off on me.

Not even the arctic wind sweeping in from the South Pole deterred me from shivering on the sidelines to watch Chris run out for Stradbroke Primary School; he was an 'in and under' player with a beautiful kick. My heart would swell as I watched him gather possessions, showing off all the skills we'd practised at home and in the park. When the game was over, we'd pile into my family's Volkswagen Beetle and talk through the highlights quarter by quarter, while Mum drove on to my playground of dreams.

All my hopes and aspirations were linked to the netball court. Smooth, potholed or asphalt, the quality of the surface didn't matter to me: for one hour every Saturday, that rectangle was my place of worship – up and down the court, attacking, defending, and creating space and opportunities. Every game was part of the grand plan. Part of what I thought was my destiny to represent the real green and gold.

'You're gonna play for Australia, Angie.'

'I know.'

Sport illuminated my childhood; it was my inspiration – not only playing it, but watching it too. If I ever lie back on a leather couch talking about my life to a bearded Austrian psychiatrist, he'll tell me that I was obsessed with my father, brother, and the green tricycle I got for my second birthday. He'll also tell me that my first true love was neither a boy nor an object, but a football club.

In September 1978, I witnessed an event that changed my life. Norwood Football Club mowed down a 29-point three-quarter time deficit to win the SANFL Grand Final by a single point. I rode every tackle, kicked every kick, screamed, booed and cheered till my voice gave up, punched the air, and cried tears of joy. That magical event took me to an emotional, sensory place that I'd never visited before: that quarter of football made me believe that anything is possible in sport – a cross I now bear.

I've had similar sporting highs over the years, and those stirring experiences are part of my lifeblood. I reach for them when I feel let down by sport; when I read about sportswomen's struggle for respect, recognition, a decent income and access to resources. At the heart of the woman I've become – a woman striving for gender equality in sport – you can still find a little girl crouching under a Hills hoist. That feisty, ambitious, energetic and free girl who cried over footy games and believed everything was achievable.

The Lone Ranger may have had Tonto by his side, but I had Chris by mine. We were like Batman and Robin (he was Robin). We connected over sport and the freedom you feel when you play it – anything that required some kind of physical activity and coordination, be it kicking footballs, shooting netballs, hula-hooping, playing hours of bocce (with coloured and battered plastic water-filled balls), running, marbles, darts, table tennis, hopping or rolling down grassy banks. My brother defined my sport-obsessed childhood.

He was there for my first serious sporting injury. At kick-to-kick in our front yard, first one, then two, then three, then most of the kids in the street turned up – ten of us hustling for position. Nine boys and me. Gentle drop punts were becoming tricky banana shots through the makeshift goals, accompanied by loud shouts of 'Watch this!' and 'Beat that!' – and then on to madly contested speckies. Determined to outshine them all (and show off to the cute Elvis look-alike next door), I leapt to the heavens, soaring well above the pack (average height: 140 centimetres), and plucked the ball out of the air ... before landing, with all the grace of a newly born elephant, on the exposed root of an ancient Moreton Bay fig tree.

My left ankle looking like a bruised water balloon, I spent the next week on the couch staring out the window: at my nemesis, the tree root. Chris waited on me hand and ankle, faithfully following instructions, preparing me cheese on biscuits and bowls of sultanas. And, at the end of the day, he'd unravel his sleeping bag on the floor next to me, and we'd chat long into the night.

*

Only much later did I come to understand the significance of what Chris and I had. At the time, of course, it didn't really mean anything to me: it just was what it was. He was my rival, confidante and hero (apart from the time he dacked me in front of mini-Elvis). What I didn't realise then was that our friendship taught me one of the most important lessons in life: the meaning of equality and mutual respect. This shaped me. Through our love of sport and all the misadventures that went with it, there was never any suggestion that my sport was of lesser value. There was never a suggestion that my sporting pursuits were somehow less worthy. There was an underlying respect between the two of us. And – even though I had three more classic catches than Chris – we truly believed that we were absolute equals.

That's why the one piece of advice I always give to high school girls is for them to bring out that invincible inner nine-year-old. I tell them: 'She represents the unrestrained you, and you're going to need her.' This is true for all areas of life, but especially for sport, because as childhood shifts into the early teenage years, any feeling of equality fades and girls begin to drop out of sport in droves.

The 2006 Senate Committee report 'About time! Women in sport and recreation in Australia' identifies a range of factors directly responsible for the low participation rates of women and girls in sport, recreation and physical activity. Some are practical (lack of time; lack of childcare and awareness of childcare options; lack of money; lack of access to appropriate, accessible and affordable facilities and services), some are personal (lack of confidence; body image issues), and others are social and cultural (social stereotyping; lack of female role models; reduced leisure time owing to family responsibilities; harassment; lack of culturally appropriate facilities or programs). This isn't peculiar to Australia: these barriers and others cause sharp drop-out rates for teenage girls worldwide. There's inequality at every level and in every sector of the sporting community, which sends the message to each generation of girls that there's no point in trying because they'll never get anywhere in sport – they won't earn as much as men, they'll never get the recognition they deserve, they'll never have a position of power, and they'll never feel as though they belong.

I was one of the lucky ones. In the golden years after my first game of netball at age eight, I was as smitten with playing sport as I was with watching it. For seven years I was fully immersed in all its goodness: friendship, healthy competition, half-time oranges and fun. So much fun. The anticipation, the preparation, the playing – and that feeling when you played well, win or lose, or if the team played well and you all got to share in the euphoria afterwards. Eventually, when I was fifteen, the realisation hit that I didn't have the talent to play for Australia, but this moment of clarity didn't stop me from playing. And I played on until the age of forty, when the thought of leaving a warm house (and forgoing a glass of shiraz) to play a 9pm game was too much to bear.

But looking back at my 'golden years' with adult eyes, I find it easy to see that whatever our abilities and whatever we believed, when it came to sporting opportunities, Chris and I were far from equals. My pathway had roadblocks that Chris's never had. Not the personal kind – my family backed me every step of the way. I didn't lack self-confidence, and my chutzpah levels went up a notch whenever I slipped the 'centre' bib over my head. I also wasn't self-conscious about my body, despite always being the shortest in the team: a small, skinny, androgynous-looking young teen with a side-flicked bouffant hairstyle that I'd rather not remember. I may have looked like the Karate Kid in a pleated netball skirt, but this never stopped me from feeling like a powerful girl. On the court, my size was my strength, not my weakness.

My roadblocks were practical and social. At the time, the media was (almost) entirely focused on men's sport. I'd heard of women who played elite sport – even football and cricket – but it's hard to aspire to be like someone that you can't see.

This sense of being invisible and excluded was reinforced by the way that my beloved sport of netball, the 'women's game', was dismissed and neglected by those in charge of community sport. Netball was something mothers did with their daughters – few fathers would appear on game day – and netball facilities always ran a very poor second to the local football and cricket facilities. We played on substandard courts: the asphalt was cracked and uneven, the lines were faded, and when there were any lights, they were never as bright as those at the footy grounds. Often there were no clubrooms – just sheds, open to the elements, with bench seats. The nearest toilet blocks were dark and dank, and it wasn't unusual for Mum's Beetle to get bogged in the rough, muddy square of the car park. Like any kid, I didn't question these inequalities, but adapted. I ran up and down potholed courts and tore strips off my knees because I loved netball. I went to the toilet in the dark and squatted above the seat because I loved netball. But the sport that I loved was clearly an afterthought for the local council. I can remember some mums grumbling about the poor facilities, but nothing ever changed; when I think about it now, it's hardly surprising that the complaints went unheard. Sporting culture itself was against us, so a few frustrated mums didn't stand a chance.

In the end, my own sporting career was cruelly cut short by a lack of talent (and a lack of height), but it didn't really make a difference. Elite sport for women seemed to be a distant and unreachable goal, or an irrelevant niche hobby, and while this didn't stop me from playing sport in my high school years, girls all around me dropped out. Some hated sport. They hated the competition, the games; they hated their bodies and what they had to wear – all the 'dorky crap'. They'd come up with the most fanciful excuses to skip PE: forged notes from their parents, fake bandages on a never-healing ankle, wrist or knee injury (sometimes they were rumbled for limping on the wrong leg!), forgotten gear, doctor's appointments and period pain (lots and lots of period pain).

I just put it down to a simple difference in taste. Not everybody likes running around. Not everybody likes to sweat.

My body was changing too, but my little teenage universe revolved around me and my group of sporty friends. I didn't think about the bigger picture of why those other girls felt uncomfortable about their bodies. That understanding came later, and it didn't come from sport.

\*

Outside of PE there was only one other class that I really loved: English. We never forget our first loves – the intensity of the emotion, the purity of it. For fifteen-year-old me that love of literature involved several books, all set in nineteenth-century England and full of the struggles of women fighting for love and rebelling against prejudice, social norms and antiquated rules and laws. When I read Jane Austen and the Brontë sisters, something stirred inside me and I couldn't get enough of them. It wasn't just their novels that I found exhilarating, but also the stories behind them – of how the Brontë sisters got published in the first place, how they had to use male pseudonyms to get their work seen and taken seriously.

Inevitably, I started to gently question my own life. In my Greek-Australian middle-class upbringing, the idea of patriarchy was never mentioned; until I started reading, I'd had no idea it even existed. But gender roles in my home were clearly defined, and Dad was the boss – not in a despotic, invading-Poland kind of way, but he was like a benevolent dictator. My family never discussed big issues around the dinner table (funnily enough, we do now).

On the surface it all worked pretty well, but my sister and I weren't allowed the freedoms that other girls had; I had a very strict curfew, and any boy seen within a two-kilometre radius of the house was shot (well, chased away – which is as good as being fired at when you're seventeen). Underneath my happy and confident exterior was a part of me that wanted to break free. It wasn't as if I put down a Jane Austen novel and screamed, '*Enough!*' then packed up my knapsack and headed off into the great unknown, but there were new rumblings inside that I was too young to fully understand.

Under the sandstone arches of the University of Adelaide, it all clicked. I discovered feminism and, for the first time, I truly felt discontent over the inequality that had been hidden beneath the surface of my childhood – I started to see things clearly, in life and sport. The dodgy courts, the sheds, the toilets, the car park, the dim lighting, the battle for court access, how much less grand our trophy presentation nights were than the boys', all those girls who hated their bodies, the drop-out rate and the lack of female role models: they were all connected.

My eyes were opened to the power imbalances between women and men, and the ongoing fight for equal rights, opportunities and respect. I found my voice and started using it for things that really mattered: Reclaim the Night marches through the streets of Adelaide; speaking out against violence; energetically arguing against sexism, double standards and inequality – at home, in the pub, whenever and wherever I got the urge.

It didn't feel all that radical back then; it just felt right. And it still does now. What could possibly be radical about wanting a better life for women? How could women not want equality, control over their bodies, the vote, equal pay and opportunities, better work conditions, better access to childcare, a world without rape and sexual harassment, and the right to feel safe inside and outside of their homes? It's not as if there's some secret agenda: 'On the first Thursday of the month, we want all men called Brian castrated.'

So it's always baffled me why the word 'feminism' whips some people up into a state of apoplexy. When I need to convince someone in sport about feminism, I ask them if they think girls should grow up with the same opportunities and pathways in sport as boys. I ask them if they think girls should be respected and valued equally with boys. I ask them if they think society should encourage girls to pursue their sporting aspirations, the same way it does for boys. As far as starting points go, I find that this works pretty well, especially when the person I'm speaking to has a daughter. It's sad that some men only start thinking about these things after they have daughters – and sad that sometimes their daughters are the only women they want to support in this way.

By the time I left uni, I felt empowered. I wasn't going to put up with any of that sexist crap. I was convinced that I would call out inequality and misogyny at every opportunity, and make the world a better place. I just didn't count on how often I'd have to do it and how hard it would be.

*

Equipped with an Honours degree in politics, a journalism degree and a love of words, I was set for a long career as a political reporter. *Elections, leadership spills and policy debate, here I come.* Or so I thought. In the ABC Adelaide newsroom where I cut my teeth, I covered a bit of everything – politics, crime, courts, sport and, as was customary for all young South

Australian reporters in the 1990s, the mating habits of greater bilbies. Because I was passionate about sport and understood it, I quickly became the back-up sports reporter, which led to a phone call from the head of news and current affairs at the ABC in Melbourne. At first a career in sports journalism didn't sound important or meaningful enough, but the more I chewed it over, the more it seemed right. I bloody loved sport, and Melbourne was the epicentre of sport in Australia, so I packed my bags and headed east. To ease my parents' pain, I said I'd only be gone a year. That was 1997.

The day I arrived, it was cold, grey and blowing a gale. Pretending not to be daunted, I made my way to the group of flats where the ABC was housing me for two weeks. I hauled my luggage up a flight of concrete stairs and, just before reaching the landing, I slipped and fell back down. Lying in a crumpled heap, I stared up at the cobwebbed entrance-hall light and wondered if this was a sign of things to come.

But as bad as my day was turning out, it wasn't as bad as Richmond coach Robert Walls's. Inside the flat, I turned on the TV just as news was breaking that Walls had been sacked by the Tigers. I watched all the live crosses, one after the other: a procession of male reporters outside Punt Road Oval telling audiences how events had unfolded. The Tigers were coming off a 137-point loss at the hands of the Adelaide Crows, which was the nail in the coffin for Walls. This was my introduction to life as a Melbourne-based sports journalist – male reporters talking about a male coach who'd supposedly failed male players and a male board.

Of course, I was already very aware that I was entering a male-dominated profession. In the sporting 'Game of Thrones', men hold sovereign power: they make the rules and call the shots. Like they have done since the beginning of time.

Fortunately, I was now able to look at the industry with a critical eye. While I've always loved sport, during my time at uni my view of it had grown from something simple and clear – classic catches by the clothesline, win/loss ratios, great goals and grand finals – into something much more complex. Sport is so deeply ingrained in our culture that it's very much part of everybody's life (whether they want it to be or not). Since uni, I've known that it can't be viewed as separate from the rest of the world – and, as such, I judge it by the standards I apply to all other parts of my life. This is why my relationship with sport is at times problematic.

*

I've been working in sport for over two decades now. And (please bear with me while I take a deep breath and raise the AP monogrammed trumpet to my lips) I have reported for programs, presented and hosted sport on television and radio. I am proud to have been the first woman to co-host a sports breakfast radio program in Melbourne. I've made a documentary called *League of Her Own* about the rise of women in Australian Rules football. I've written for newspapers and online publications on a wide range of sports and, more recently, on the cultural side of sport.

The point I'm making is that I've been around sport for a heck of a long time. And the observations I make come from experience.

Sports media is a boys' club. I've seen men with mediocre talent get jobs ahead of more talented women time and time again, just because they're men. I've even been on the receiving end of it once or twice. But there has been progress: while women sports journos were once as rare as the Northern hairy-nosed wombat, you can now find them across the spectrum of TV, radio, print and online. You'll even see and hear the odd one with the right to an opinion on sport panel shows – but rarely more than one. One woman shows that we're doing *something* to tackle this whopping gender gap: more than one would indicate something like real progress.

Over the years, my love for sport has been severely tested, and on more than one occasion I've felt like walking away. But I never do.

The treatment of women in sport has always bothered me, but only now do I feel I have the runs on the board to do something about it. Listening to the struggles of women athletes and hearing the same stories over and over again – the lack of respect, lack of recognition, lack of a pathway and lack of money – motivated me to take a good hard look at the Australian sporting scene. Those women are the driving force behind this book. But it's not just about female athletes. It's about *all* women in sport: athletes, administrators, journalists, presenters, fans and young girls – especially the girls.

Most fair-minded people have had enough of the objectification of sportswomen in the media and are tired of sexist 'jokes'. We're all sickened when we hear of yet another sexual assault being handled badly by sports authorities. Elements like these have cast dark shadows over the Australian sporting landscape.

Thankfully, I'm wired a particular way – I'm an optimist (thanks to that 1978 SANFL Grand Final). I believe that culture can change for the good. We can all change our attitudes to create a better, safer and more equal society for everyone – inside and outside of sport. It's a whole lot easier to get things done as an optimist. We're more likely to hide veggies in pasta sauce believing that our child will fall in love with broccoli. When the petrol gauge drops below 'E', we think we can still squeeze another trip or two out of the car. We're the AFL fans who circle, with relish, at least fourteen wins when the fixture comes out. We're the ones who believe we can come back from twenty-nine points down at three-quarter time.

In her last public appearance as Australia's sex discrimination commissioner, Elizabeth Broderick said: 'A life without advocating for change is not a life that will have meaning for me.' As far as stealing other people's mantras goes, this is a good one.

My connection to sport will always be with me. I am a fan. I'll turn up to support my team come rain, hail or shine. I lament poor umpiring decisions. I let out primal screams. I hide in the laundry when scores are level with forty-five seconds left on the clock. I go into lockdown for a week after a finals loss – if it's by less than a kick, you may not see me down at the shops for a month. I won't rest until my son is fully indoctrinated into the Adelaide Crows tribe, and I'll work just as tirelessly to turn him against his father's sporting allegiance to England.

But as much as I'm still a fan, and a nightmare one at times, I see sport for what it is – underneath all the gloss and hoopla is an overtly masculine empire that needs a radical makeover to get with the times.

When you put together the evidence, this is very plain to see.

# 2

## THIS IS A MAN'S WORLD

If sport were a cake, the filling would be chest hair.

*Me*

One question has doggedly followed me throughout my career as a sports journalist:

'Do you like sport?'

It's always asked with a slightly puzzled look. *Can it be true? That you really like sport? You're a – y'know, you don't have a … or a set of … You're a woman! How would you get it?*

Burdened with a polite nature, I've never done what I really should do to that question: pick it up and send it, with a perfectly executed drop punt, back to 1953.

This kind of sexism runs deep in sport. From the seemingly innocuous throwaway line between mates to deeper, more ingrained issues such as pay inequality, lack of media coverage, sexploitation and even abuse. Sport's long history of sexism is so ingrained that we can't magically erase the bias by talking up the successes of women athletes and creating new competitions for elite sportswomen. We have to go further than that.

Admittedly, as a sports journalist, being asked whether I like sport or not sits at the lower end of the offence scale, but casual sexism is just one part of the problem – the outer layer that can be seen, heard and challenged straight away. Underneath, buried deep in sport's foundations, is something much harder to confront. Elizabeth Broderick calls it 'gender asbestos': 'It's built into the walls, the floors, the ceilings of institutions and organisations, the behaviours, the practices. It's often not tangible.' Gender asbestos has many guises in sport, all insidiously working to prevent women from achieving equality in both the field of play and the boardroom.

*

Sport has been typically considered a male pursuit for as long as men have been playing with their balls. When Ancient Greece introduced formal sports in 776 BC, the male participants competed in the nude for all to see their 'masculinity'. Slaves and women weren't permitted to compete, and married women were also barred from watching the Olympics (maidens, prostitutes and the priestess of Demeter were allowed to attend). As a result, women were forced to develop their own competition, the Games of Hera, and the separation between male and female sport was set – with the male version dominating across the board.

Fast forward to the present day, and not much has changed. In identifying the key barriers that stop women from participating in sport, the Australian Sports Commission's Clearinghouse for

Sport noted in March 2016 that a big problem is the maleness of the culture:

> Although social attitudes toward participation by females in sport activities have changed dramatically over time, the predominant social 'view' of sport, as portrayed in print and electronic media, is still male-oriented. Research supports the fact that very few differences exist between the participation patterns and attitudes of boys and girls under the age of twelve years. However, as girls mature there are social and cultural, and perhaps biological, considerations that impact upon their decision to participate in sport during adolescence and throughout life.

Sport is still mainly by men, for men, and everything that happens in and around the industry reinforces that idea. The men in charge sit around oblong mahogany tables surrounded by the faces of more men, hanging on the walls in heavy gilt frames. Under the gaze of their forefathers, the men at the table know that they have a duty of care to protect their sport's history. Tradition, goddammit, ensures that the game is safeguarded by trusted men, preserving the ancient ways that have held them in good stead for generations … Now, pass around the port and cigars.

Australian sporting culture is what it is because of its traditions and customs, as is sporting culture throughout much of the world. Now, I'm all for tradition and customs – I had the local Greek priest drop by and bless my new house with prayers and sprinklings of holy water to rid every room of evil and, being a fan of *The Exorcist*, I found the whole thing oddly reassuring – but I'm not for traditions and customs that exclude sections of society.

Golf clubs have been doing this for centuries. In 2012, Augusta National Golf Club, home to the most prestigious golf tournament in the world, the Masters, finally welcomed its first female members eighty years after its founding, having caved in to a campaign spearheaded by Martha Burk of the National Council of Women's Organizations. The first two women invited to join were former Secretary of State Condoleezza Rice and South Carolina financier Darla Moore. (Rice's invitation is even more poignant when you consider that Augusta National didn't invite its first African-American member until 1990.) The Royal and Ancient Golf Club of St Andrews admitted women as members in 2014 – 260 years after it was founded. These changes can take considerable planning.

Conversely, in May 2016, Muirfield Golf Club in Scotland voted to continue its policy of excluding women – the vote came back 64 per cent for and 36 per cent against changing the membership rules, just short of a required two-thirds majority. A group of about thirty members wrote anonymously to fellow golfers before the ballot, urging them to reject the change. The letter argued that 'the introduction of lady members is bound to create difficulties', and that the presence of women would 'endanger foursomes and speedy play'.

Cricket has been a merry dance for men too. Speaking at an International Women's Day breakfast in 2015, Cricket Australia CEO James Sutherland took aim at his sport's failure to include women:

Despite the long history, it is fair to say cricket has been conservative and generally reluctant to promote female involvement in the game. In some parts, cricket has deserved the suggestion that it was predominantly 'pale, male and stale'. Whilst slow to get going, we are now determined to make up for lost time.

For more than a century, the Lord's Pavilion at the Marylebone Cricket Club (MCC) had a men-only rule during the hours of play – the only woman permitted to enter the Pavilion during play was Queen Elizabeth II. In *Skirting the Boundary: A History of Women's Cricket,* Isabelle Duncan tells: 'At a Special General Meeting held for members at Lord's on 24 February 1998 to tackle, once again, the issue of "lady membership"', one member just couldn't shake his concerns about atmospherics:

> If we were debating tonight whether to have fruit machines in the Long Room, I would vote against it because it would alter the atmosphere of the Club. If we were debating whether to wear shorts in hot weather and take off our shirts, I would vote against it because it would alter the atmosphere of the Club. Likewise, as the Committee say, having lady members would alter the atmosphere of the Club.

MCC President Tony Lewis described the process of persuading almost eighteen thousand members as 'like turning an ocean-going liner through 180 degrees', but in 1999 the Lord's Pavilion finally opened its doors to women. Similarly, the Long Room at the Melbourne Cricket Ground was a no-go zone for women until 1984.

Historically, golf and cricket members really have needed a member to get in.

Away from the perfectly rectangular cucumber sandwiches and jugs of Pimm's, traditions have also restricted (and continue to restrict) women athletes in a range of other sports.

Remarkably, there's still no women's race at the most prestigious cycling event of them all – the Tour de France. You'll see 120 women in Paris as a warm-up act before the men ride in to complete their final stage at the Arc de Triomphe. The men will have raced around 3500 kilometres, twenty-one stages spread across three weeks; the women's La Course by Le Tour de France is just one 89-kilometre stage.

In 2013, Beijing Olympics road-cycling champion Nicole Cooke used her retirement speech to highlight the blatant sexism in cycling:

> At the age of twelve, one is unaware of the problems ahead. One expects there to be an infrastructure for both boys and girls to develop and demonstrate their talents; to nurture them. One does not expect that nothing is available if you are a girl or, that worse still, girls will be specifically excluded, not allowed to compete. It is somewhat of a handicap trying to demonstrate just how good you are on a bike when you are not allowed to ride.

And cycling isn't the only long-distance sport that's had problems in this area. In 1967, Kathrine Switzer transformed marathon running for women. She surreptitiously entered the

Boston Marathon using her initials ('KV' Switzer) when women were officially banned from participating. During the event, race director Jock Semple tried to rip her race number off and have her ejected; he grabbed her shoulders and shouted, 'Get the hell out of my race and give me those numbers!' Nonetheless, in a time of four hours and twenty minutes, Switzer became the first woman to officially complete the Boston Marathon. News of her feat – and confrontation with Semple – spread worldwide. Back then, the common thinking (mostly among men) was that women couldn't run long distances without doing harm to their reproductive systems or their fragile psyches. David Epstein, author of *The Sports Gene: Inside the Science of Extraordinary Athletic Performance*, puts it very clearly:

> There is no doubt that there are important physical differences between men and women. They range from men's denser bones [which can support more muscle], taller stature, longer proportional limbs, to more oxygen-carrying red-blood cells. That, of course, is why we separate men and women for the purposes of competition. But the short answer is: there's no good reason that women don't have the events that men do.

Although Switzer changed the world for women distance runners, some sexist traditions in athletics remain: for example, the men's decathlon has been contested at every Olympics since 1912, but there's still no place at major championships for the women's event. Meanwhile, in swimming, there's no women's 1500-metre freestyle at the Olympics – it's held at the World and European Championships, but the best long-distance female swimmers rarely compete. Why would they put all that effort into training for a non-Olympic event? In gymnastics, women compete in four apparatus (vault, uneven bars, balance beam and floor) while men compete in six. There's no four-woman bobsleigh at the Winter Olympics, and there are more weight divisions in Olympic men's boxing, wrestling and weightlifting than in the women's side of the sport. (Women's boxing didn't become an Olympic event until 2012, despite first appearing alongside men's boxing as a demonstration sport at the 1904 St Louis Olympic Games.)

*

The concept of gender is instilled in us from birth and is nearly impossible to shake. If you're in need of some Gender Studies 101, here's the lowdown: stereotypes around what traits are 'male' and 'female' lead to the creation of gender roles. Men are big, strong, competitive, determined and assertive – traits known as 'masculine'; women are soft, gentle, nurturing and kind – traits known as 'feminine'. Society latches on to these traditional gender roles, and they seep into the way we think, the way we act and the value we place on those around us.

The unconscious brain processes an astonishing 200,000 times more information than the conscious brain, and unconscious bias occurs when untested messages – for instance, about gender – are accepted as truth. The attitudes and behaviours that keep sporting culture so male-dominated are propped up by a mixture of unconscious *and* conscious biases, which influences recruitment and selection decisions, and keeps the same men around the oblong mahogany table. It's not only men who show unconscious bias, either: our aspirations tend to reflect current norms, and with relatively few women in key roles in sport, other women find themselves doubting their abilities and holding back. This isn't to say that gender roles always go unchallenged – in fact, these roles are continually tested and reshaped – but, for the most part, the stereotypes have stayed much the same throughout history.

Gender roles have become part of sporting vernacular, a frequent reminder of the voice of the past shaping the present. In playgrounds and parks across the country, boys tell other boys to 'man up' when they look sad, while unsporty kids are nailed with lines such as, 'Stop playing like a bunch of girls.' A bad miss is usually followed by, 'My mum could kick better than that.' (Or, as I've heard my partner say while watching his beloved Sunderland in the English Premier League, 'My grandmother could kick better than that, and she's been dead for thirty years!')

All these seemingly innocuous sayings have power – and if you think that I'm over-reaching, you should google #LikeAGirl. What you'll find is a genius social experiment. Its YouTube video (part of the larger #LikeAGirl campaign by feminine hygiene brand Always) recruited real women, men, teenagers, and pre-pubescent boys and girls, and asked them to show what it physically meant to run like a girl, throw like a girl and fight like a girl. The results were incredible. The pre-pubescent girls performed these actions confidently and proudly, while all the older participants performed them in a frivolous, self-deprecating manner. At a certain point, women begin to internalise all the negative connotations that come from doing things 'like a girl' – in other words, they start believing the bullshit. The only way to bury our hidden biases is to unlearn current beliefs and relearn new ones.

When you add conscious bias to the mix – discrimination, gender stereotypes, ignorance and nepotism – it's hardly surprising that there's a conspicuous sameness to the Australian sporting landscape that's reflected in administration, coaching, umpiring, sports medicine and the Fox Footy wardrobe department on game day.

*

Casual sexism reinforces the well-established notion that women are inferior. When it comes to women's sport, this kind of sexism is often contained in any or all of the following statements: 'Women's sport is boring.' 'Women's sport is less exciting to watch.' 'It's just not as physical.' 'They look like men.' 'They're all dykes.' 'Why would I pay to see that?'

For a snapshot of this kind of elevated thinking, head to the online comments section at the bottom of any piece about women and sport. The lamprey that hangs off the story's underbelly, this section provides a great outlet for frustrated people who want a voice. The anonymity of the internet gives them the freedom to unleash the full force of their insight. Fuelled by the sniff of any kind of positivity in a story on women's sport, they're off. Lights dimmed, curtains drawn and – pause for thought, because this is important, this is their message – followed by a slow finger jabbing at the keyboard, *tap, tap, tap* … :

'Women's sport is shit.'

This depressing little sentence is by far the most frequent of these online comments.

The popular default position of this kind of thinker is an insistence on comparing women's sport with men's. People who bang on like this firmly believe that men are the measuring stick of greatness. Even those who choose to frame their argument a bit less bluntly insist on toeing a very blinkered party line (and by the careful insertion of 'no offence', are clearly made reasonable): 'No offence, but women aren't as strong as men, they're not as fast as men, they're not as skilful as men, they're not as aggressive, they're just not as good, and if they were as good they'd be competing with men.'

Stop right there. I'm getting a flashback to the gold-coated rickshaw that carried Bobby Riggs (in his yellow Sugar Daddy jacket) onto court to play against Billie Jean King in tennis's 1973 'Battle of the Sexes', and it's not pretty. For the record, King won the match in straight sets, 6–4, 6–3, 6–3 – but this was pure pantomime.

In general, pitting women against men isn't the answer; that's a circus, not sport. The obvious genetic differences should be embraced and not matched against one another to prove a dubious point. If Usain Bolt beats Elaine Thompson in a sprint race, does this mean that reigning Olympic champion Thompson isn't fast? The cheetah is faster than the gazelle, but we don't think of the gazelle as a slouch. Are male gymnasts stronger then female gymnasts? Yes. But are they as graceful? The comparisons become mind-numbingly stupid.

To assume that contests involving power and speed are better to watch than those that showcase grace and skill is a pretty one-eyed way to look at things. For lovers of boxing, it's like saying that I'm only interested in watching heavyweight Mike Tyson fight – Sugar Ray Leonard as a welterweight wasn't exciting to watch because he wasn't powerful enough. Women's sport is physically different to men's, but that doesn't make it any less strategic or passionate; in fact, you could argue that relying less on brute force puts more of an emphasis on tactics and strategy, making it more of a spectacle – well, certainly a more nuanced spectacle. Anyway, beauty and skill are in the eye of the beholder: where some people see two highly trained, dedicated professional athletes executing unbelievable hand-eye coordination under intense pressure, others see a couple of fat blokes throwing darts at a fancy-dress party.

Equality is about being valued for who you are, not being forced to take on the characteristics of others. Thank god we're different: the world would be a boring place if we weren't. Let's embrace our differences and appreciate them for what they are.

As for women's sport being dull, I've sat through a lot of sport for work and pleasure, and I can categorically state that women don't have a monopoly on boring. I've been close to comatose on many, many occasions watching men's sport. I've dozed off during many Formula One Grand Prix races, golf rounds and baseball games – and, I swear, my heart actually stopped beating during New Zealander Geoff Allott's 77-ball duck against South Africa in 1999. This isn't to say that these sports are boring, but they do sometimes offer up action so singularly devoid of action that watching them becomes less about following the sport and more about maintaining the will to live.

The only thing boring about women's sport is the need for it to be continually defended against biased perceptions. *Yawn*. Female athletes are well used to being seen as less strong, less fast, less interesting – and just plain less – than their male counterparts. They've heard it all before.

Casual sexism also has an evangelical preoccupation with what women athletes look like. These online commenters show the same kind of enthusiasm for women's couture that I had as a fourteen-year-old watching a punk-glam Madonna sail down Venetian canals singing 'Like a Virgin'. The underlying message here is: it's okay to run around and play sport, but it's much better if you look 'hot' too. Just being an athlete isn't enough.

If these preconceived ideas about women's sport and sportswomen only belonged to keyboard warriors, it wouldn't be so bad, but they also influence decisions made throughout the sporting community. Casual sexism is an industry issue, one with consequences that affect everyone who loves sport.

For a glimpse of that unwavering commitment to old-fashioned notions of femininity, let's take a look at a few examples (there are plenty to choose from), starting with former AFL coach (and SANFL player) Graham Cornes. In 2015, after watching the AFL women's exhibition game between Melbourne and the Western Bulldogs at the MCG, he said, 'It just didn't look right! ... Perhaps it was the outfits ... Not particularly flattering ... most of them looked like girls playing football. Boobs and all.' Searing insights, Cornsey. They looked like girls playing football because they were indeed girls and, yes, they were playing football. As for it not looking right, and as for the boobs, beauty certainly is in the eye of the beholder.

Disgraced FIFA boss Sepp Blatter said that in order to make women's soccer more popular, officials should 'let the women play in more feminine clothes like they do in volleyball. They could, for example, have tighter shorts.' Sepp, you're a genius. Why wear shorts at all?

And here's what BBC commentator John Inverdale said about Marion Bartoli after she was crowned 2013 Wimbledon champion:

> I just wonder if her dad, because he has obviously been the most influential person in her life, did say to her when she was twelve, thirteen, fourteen, maybe, 'Listen, you are never going to be, you know, a looker. You are never going to be somebody like a Sharapova, you're never going to be 5 foot 11, you're never going to be somebody with long legs, so you have to compensate for that. You are going to have to be the most dogged, determined fighter that anyone has ever seen on the tennis court if you are going to make it.' And she kind of is.

Inverdale later blamed bad hay fever for his comments.

Casual sexism also likes a scapegoat of the female kind. Over the years, I've heard some bizarre excuses for a team underperforming, but none more hilarious than one circulated by Ian Healy. In a desperate attempt to explain why Australia was bowled out for 60 in just 111 balls before lunch on day one of the 2015 Fourth Ashes Test, Healy pointed his finger at the WAGs. Oddly, I don't recall any of the players' wives or girlfriends pulling on the pads that day in Nottingham and striding out to the crease – admittedly, it was late when I was watching, but I'm pretty sure I hadn't nodded off. Healy's argument was that women are a distraction for elite sportsmen; in order to allow their men to focus, they – and any accompanying children – should be invisible. Apparently, any reminder of life and responsibilities outside the dressing-room is just too much for male cricketers to handle.

My partner's argument for the Australian capitulation was a little more succinct: 'They're crap, Ange.'

You may also enjoy these words of wisdom from tennis player Jo-Wilfried Tsonga:

> You know, the girls, they are more unstable emotionally than us. I'm sure everybody will say it's true, even the girls … it's just about hormones and all this stuff. [Men] don't have all these bad things, so we are physically in a good shape every time and you are not. That's it.

Tsonga's thesis on 'The Effects of Women's Hormones and Stuff' is being submitted to *La Revue de Médecine Interne* next year.

\*

Too often, casual sexism is dismissed as a joke or a throwaway line. When AFL legend Billy Brownless was called out for announcing, 'Here come the strippers!' over a microphone as a woman and her eighteen-year-old daughter passed through the junior footy function he was hosting, there was an outpouring of sympathy for Brownless. The usual cries of political correctness gone mad filled the airwaves: 'That's just Billy, he's a larrikin.' The good old Larrikin Defence is a favourite of those who indulge in this kind of humour, but while there's something charming about the Australian larrikin attitude, which writers and poets have romanticised for years, it has a darker side – it camouflages and subtly reinforces sexism, racism and homophobia. At the time, Brownless said that his remark was a 'throwaway line': 'I didn't mean anything by it.' And I'm sure that he didn't. Unfortunately, he said it, and it was very hurtful and humiliating for the woman and her daughter. Just as Australian tennis player Nick Kyrgios' 'Kokkinakis banged your girlfriend, sorry to tell you that, mate' was a throwaway line, and West Indian cricketer Chris Gayle's on-air propositioning of (visibly cringing) sports reporter Mel McLaughlin was capped off with the throwaway line: 'Don't blush, baby.'

Eddie McGuire's on-air suggestion that he'd pay to drown journalist Caroline Wilson, an idea enthusiastically taken up by his radio colleagues James Brayshaw and Danny Frawley, put this kind of sexism firmly on the map in 2016. I've known McGuire for many years and I wouldn't describe him as sexist. But this example demonstrated just how innate sexist language and 'banter' is among men (in sport) – and, as unsavoury as it was, it generated lots of discussion about the links between casual sexism and attitudes that support violence against women. It also severely dented the 'poor attempt at humour' defence.

Not all poorly-thought-out comments are clearly offensive. Sometimes gender asbestos shows itself in surprising places, through casual sexism that's well meant and can even appear supportive of women. When the England women's football team had finished its 2015 World Cup campaign, this is how the official Football Association Twitter account, which had almost 1.2 million followers at the time, welcomed the players home: 'Our #Lionesses go back to being mothers, partners and daughters today, but they have taken on another title – heroes.' The tweet was quickly deleted, following criticism on social media, but many people didn't understand why it was described as 'sexist' and 'patronising'. Of course, the FA never meant for it to come across like that, but to me the message was clear: women's roles as mothers, partners and daughters are incompatible with stellar international careers. Apply the 'Would you tweet that about the men's team?' test, and the answer is obvious. This comment is particularly damaging because of the uncomfortable relationship between motherhood and elite sport – the industry rarely gets it right when it comes to support for mothers.

When you stack throwaway line on top of throwaway line, sexist 'joke' on top of sexist 'joke', and sprinkle well-intentioned sexism over all of it, you've soon got a pile the size of Everest and a systemic pattern of behaviour. Children see and hear this behaviour and think that it's the norm; they then repeat what they see and hear – and the cycle continues. When attitudes like these go unchecked, sexism breeds like bacteria in a Petri dish: 'Women's sport is a waste of time.' 'Ladies don't belong in our club.' 'Girls can't kick.' I've been watching the misogynists closely, year after year, and there's a small part of me that sort of admires their resilience – in the same way that I admire cockroaches and ticks. (Did you know that ticks can live for years without drinking blood before they eventually starve to death …?)

Although things have changed since the days of Fanny Blankers-Koen (who won four gold medals in track and field at the 1948 Olympics and, because she was a mother of two, was called 'The Flying Housewife'), sport is largely built on sexist assumptions – and some of these assumptions, like red wine spilt on a cream carpet, are extremely hard to shift.

# 3

---

# THE CHICKEN AND
# THE EGG

It could be any one of a hundred Friday lunchtime events celebrating sport. On the panel, on stage, four of us (I'm the only woman) are sharing personal stories about sport: our career highlights, most emotional moments and brushes with super-famous sportspeople – did they live up to our expectations or did they disappoint?

I'm perched precariously on a high swivel stool, my leopard-print heels searching for the footrest, but after a few futile attempts it becomes clear that without elastic powers my feet aren't going to reach the bottom. I curse the organisers. The Elaine Benes voice inside my head mutters, 'A stool is not a chair!'

The discussion turns to the lack of coverage of women's sport. Then he begins: 'It's a "chicken and egg" situation ...'

And that sentence, like Pavlov's bell, is my cue to drift off and formulate my shopping list for the way home: *Nappies, wipes, eggs, avocados, pears ...*

I can see that his mouth's still moving, a clear sign he's still motoring.

*Milk, wine, definitely wine …*

My media colleague on the panel is banging on about a major problem faced by women in sport: the public, sponsors and advertisers usually don't show much interest in women's sport, so the media chooses to ignore it; the media chooses to ignore women's sport, so women's sport struggles to gain interest from the public, sponsors and advertisers.

Whenever someone brings up this topic, out comes the poultry metaphor: 'What came first, the chicken or the egg?' If I had a dollar for every time some effortless know-all has told me (with a look of smug resignation) that the lack of coverage of women's sport is a 'chicken-and-egg situation' and 'there's nothing you can do', I'd be living in a restored medieval castle in the south of France with a three Michelin star chef and a fully stocked cellar of Penfolds Grange. The only chicken I'd care about is the free-range one that Jean-Paul (my semi-naked fantasy chef) would stuff with fresh herbs, porcini and pancetta butter.

But just in case you've managed to get to this point in your life without being expertly cornered by one of those chicken-and-egg theorists, let me explain what it *really* means in relation to women's sport:

It's a vicious cycle, and one that's very difficult for women in sport to break. If women's sport attracted more interest, then media outlets and sponsors say they'd invest more time and money in covering them. With more sponsorships and media coverage, women's events would draw in more viewers … Are you getting a headache?

The answer – like the answers to all the questions raised in this book – lies in the cultural norms that shape the way we act and think. The media and sponsors are influential and powerful beasts created by our society, not detached entities making decisions in a vacuum; as such, they're just as influenced by stereotypes and perceptions as the rest of us. Pushing the chicken-and-egg dismissal lets the media and sponsors off the hook by giving them an easy out: 'People just don't care enough about women's sport.' 'The market never lies.' 'We're not in the business of propping up sports.' 'We're not here to act as cheerleaders for women's sport.' 'We're all about commercial gain.' That's what you'll hear, rather than an informed discussion about the reasons why women's sport is 'less popular' than men's sport and a serious conversation about whether we all think women's sport matters.

The circular chicken-and-egg argument stops people from looking for solutions and actively changing things to help girls and women succeed. The bottom line remains – there's much less media coverage, sponsorship and income for sportswomen.

\*

Women have certainly had to fight for their place in sport. When Baron Pierre de Coubertin resurrected the modern Olympics in 1896, not much had changed from Ancient Greek times: women were still excluded from participating. The Baron was particularly offended by the thought of a woman sweating, as described in Mary Leigh's 'Pierre de Coubertin: A man of his time': 'Indecency, ugliness, and impropriety were strong reasons, in Coubertin's view, for excluding women from the Olympic Games. His aesthetic sense was shocked by the sight of lightly clad, sweating women engaged in strenuous activity.'

The Baron sounds like an absolute barrel of laughs, and he wasn't alone in harbouring some very strange views. Some nineteenth-century doctors believed that menstruation and reproduction were so exhausting that women could not (and should not) participate in physical exercise. Sitting on a bicycle was 'said to induce menstruation and cause contracted vaginas and collapsed uteri' – not to mention deplete the energy needed to conceive and bear healthy children.

Although women are happily riding around on bikes with their uteri still intact, disciples of the Baron walk among us – and some of them work in the media. They may not show the same aversion to sweaty women, but by upholding the view that sport is, and always will be, primarily a male pursuit, the media pushes a dangerous untruth.

All you need to do is thumb through the pages of any major newspaper or switch on the radio or television on weekends to see how wildly unequal the situation is. If that's not scientific enough for you, there's a mountain of research – Australian and international – on the issue of media coverage and portrayal of sportswomen. Since 1980, this research has indicated that women struggle to get consistent, long-term and supportive media attention.

A study called 'Towards a Level Playing Field: Sport and Gender in Australian Media' (2010) found that television coverage of women's sport had declined markedly over the previous decade, from 11 per cent to just 7.4 per cent. This was despite 'the ongoing successes and strong participation levels of women in sport'. The study also found that coverage of men's sport made up 81 per cent of TV sports bulletins, compared to women's sport at 8.7 per cent: 'To put this into context, horse racing received more air time than women's sport in Australian television news.'

| Gender | Overall | ABC | SBS | Seven | Nine | Ten |
|--------|---------|-----|-----|-------|------|-----|
| Male sport | 81.1% | 80.7% | 84.8% | 81.4% | 78.9% | 80.9% |
| Female sport | 8.7% | 11.2% | 8.9% | 7.8% | 7.4% | 8.6% |
| Other | 7.4% | 5.1% | 3.5% | 8.6% | 9.4% | 7.9% |
| Mixed | 2.8% | 3% | 2.7% | 2.2% | 4.2% | 2.6% |

Source: 'Towards a Level Playing Field: Sport and Gender in Australian Media'

A more recent Australian Sports Commission (ASC) report – the *Women in Sport Broadcasting Analysis Final Report* (April 2014) – found that there was no change in the proportion of women's dedicated TV coverage since 2008 (7 per cent), 70 per cent of all female coverage was broadcast on pay TV, and tennis accounted for nearly half (47 per cent) of all dedicated female sport coverage on TV. Here's the breakdown of women's sport coverage across traditional and new media platforms over three waves:

| | Feb 2014 | Nov 2013 | July 2013 |
|--|----------|----------|-----------|
| TV News | 5% | 4% | 8% |
| Print News | 7% | 5% | 7% |
| Online News | 3% | 3% | 6% |
| Social Media | 4% | 8% | 26% |

Source: 'Women in Sport Broadcasting Analysis Final Report'

And it's interesting to note that the July 2013 spike in social media coverage coincided with the sexism row that erupted after John Inverdale's comments about Marion Bartoli.

As shocking as the ASC's findings are, they've come as no surprise to Charles Sturt University researcher Dr Chelsea Litchfield, who's been researching the issue for many years. She says that these figures are representative of many studies that have been carried out in the past, particularly in the United States, the United Kingdom and Australia. Dr Litchfield and her CSU colleague Dr Jaquelyn Osborne conducted their own research into newspaper coverage of gendered sports between 2008 and 2012. Their study, 'Women in the Sports Pages: A brief insight into Olympic and non-Olympic years in Australia', compared the coverage that women received during Olympic years (2008, 2012) and non-Olympic years (2009, 2010 and 2011) in the *Australian*, the *Sydney Morning Herald* and the *Daily Telegraph*: 'Our study showed that during non-Olympic years, the coverage of female athletes was around 4 per cent and during the Olympics it was around 14 per cent. Animal sports accounted for an average of 8.5 per cent of coverage during these periods.'

It's disheartening and completely unacceptable that, over a decade and despite the strides made by women in almost every other part of society, there's been so little improvement in the coverage of women's sport – in some cases, it's gone backwards. The things that we tell ourselves about why women's sport still lacks support and resources are all excuses and not solutions. A whole lot of people, not just in the media, should be doing more to paint an accurate picture of what's happening with women and sport in Australia.

In the latest Australian Bureau of Statistics study on 'Participation in Sport and Physical Recreation, Australia 2013–14', an estimated 60 per cent of the adult population (aged fifteen years and older) reported that they'd participated in some form of sport or physical recreation during the twelve months prior to the interview. The overall participation rate by gender was 61 per cent (males) and 59 per cent (females). More girls are taking up non-traditional sports like Australian Rules, soccer, rugby league and cricket, and women and girls are connecting with sport through social media. It's taken a while, but finally some sports have figured out that if you engage with women as both players and spectators, you stand to win big time – the AFL, soccer and cricket have been doing this, and women's participation rates are soaring. Meanwhile, the sports media has been slow to pick up on this and needs to change its mindset.

Interestingly, the ASC's 'Women in Sport Broadcasting' report found that, on average, male consumed about ninety-seven minutes of women's sport each week while females consumed ninety-two minutes each week. Newsflash: both men and women are interested in women's sport!

The ASC's report also found that while both consumers and industry members admit that more women's sport should be covered through traditional media channels in Australia, networks look at each sport and each sporting event on its merits, and viewership and interest are broadcasters' key decision drivers. John O'Sullivan, Fox's chief operating officer, said: 'Commercial networks will view a sport irrespective of the gender on its merits. Our decision is based on the quality of the coverage and the size of the population of the sport playing.'

Justin Holdforth, ABC TV's head of sports and events, believes that, 'If there is no audience interest in these things then you go, well, why aren't we investing our finite resources into something actually that people are interested in?'

But these arguments fail to recognise the key role that social conditioning and stereotyping play in shaping our perceptions of women's sport. They also don't consider the role that the media plays in this. Cheryl Cooky, an associate professor at Purdue University and one of the authors of '"It's Dude Time!": A Quarter Century of Excluding Women's Sports in Televised News and Highlight Shows', explains:

> Men's sports are going to seem more exciting, they have higher production values, higher-quality coverage, and higher-quality commentary ... When you watch women's sports, and there are fewer camera angles, fewer cuts to shot, fewer instant replays, yeah, it's going to seem to be a slower game, [and] it's going to seem to be less exciting.

Television executives say that it's not their responsibility to champion any sport and will talk up market forces till their heads explode. I get that they need to make money, but how is a sport expected to generate a commercial return if the public isn't given a chance to see it? How can women's sport find an audience if it's never on free-to-air television? The media plays a crucial role here: you create interest by putting stories in the paper, showing women athletes in action on TV, and having conversations and debates about women's sport wherever and whenever you can. This is how athletes become household names; this is how you get bums on seats; this is how you get eyeballs in front of the box – advertiser revenue is tied to viewer ratings, and viewer ratings are shaped by media coverage. So, the argument that media won't cover women's sports until there's an audience ignores its own role in creating those audiences. As the saying goes, 'If you build it, they will come.'

*

The way that women in sport are covered in the media is steeped in age-old, industrial-strength stereotypes, and this contributes to the sense that they don't deserve serious media coverage for their athletic achievements. Often, their homemaking skills come first.

Imagine this as an article headline: 'Married father of three, John Worsfold, has been appointed Essendon coach for three years.' The truth is, it would never happen – a man in sport, or any other profession for that matter, would never be defined by his relationship or family status. These things certainly wouldn't be mentioned before his coaching credentials: the actual qualities that got him the job. Nor should they be.

In 2014, Peta Searle signed with St Kilda as a development coach. This was a very big deal. Women have slowly been climbing the AFL's executive ladder but never before had a woman muscled her way into the coaching ranks.

Searle's appointment sent a powerful message to girls that coaching at the elite level of football is possible. You can crack the boys' club if you're good enough (and blessed with truckloads of resilience and humour). The usual suspects – the ragers who foam at the mouth on talkback radio and clog websites with their fury – couldn't wait to let rip: 'It's tokenism in the extreme.' 'What is happening to our great game?' 'Go back to netball.' 'What the fuck would she know?' 'What's next, women playing AFL?'

Unquestionably, Searle got the job on merit. As head coach of the Darebin Falcons in the Victorian Women's Football League, she led the club to five consecutive premierships. She was the first woman coach in the TAC Cup Under 18 Competition, an assistant to Gary Ayres at Port Melbourne in the VFL, and she represented Victoria at state level. On top of all this, she's a qualified teacher. But despite her long list of credentials, some media reports highlighted Searle's status as a 'single mother of two' before anything else. That's exactly how *Women's Health* magazine presented the story: 'This is Peta Searle. She's a single mum from Melbourne who is leaving her job as a primary school teacher to take up a new position as St Kilda Football Club's assistant coach: it's the highest position ever held by a female in the AFL.' It should have read: 'This is Peta Searle. She's a five-time premiership-winning coach of Darebin in the VWFL and former assistant coach at Port Melbourne.'

So, is it relevant that Searle is a single mother of two? Only in the context of her struggle to stay in the football system. She walked away from her VFL job to return to teaching; she couldn't justify renewing her contract of $5000 – and this is where a reference to her private life makes sense. Referring to her at the beginning of a story as a single mother of two shifts the focus away from football and diminishes her achievement.

'But it's the point of difference,' a male colleague exclaimed while we were debating the different ways that the media describes men and women in sport.

'No, the fact she's a woman is the point of difference,' I replied.

That's what should be celebrated and discussed, not the blindly gendered details of her personal life. She's not the first-ever coach to have kids or a job outside of sport, or the first coach to work in education.

Women have been defined this way since St Helena Augusta. (From an ancient scroll: 'Helena, ex-wife of Emperor Constantius, a proud single mum and keen embroiderer, is about to put down her needle and turn her mind to church-building'.) It feeds into the nurturing stereotype that serves the patriarchy well. I'm not suggesting the media does it consciously to keep the wheels of patriarchy turning; it's just that usual unconscious bias.

\*

Woman as nurturer isn't the only lazy stereotype that gets a good run in the media. After her straight-sets win over Kiki Bertens of the Netherlands at the 2015 Australian Tennis Open, Eugenie Bouchard was asked by the on-court interviewer, Ian Cohen, to 'give us a twirl and tell us about your outfit'.

'A twirl?' replied the seventh seed, slightly bemused.

'A twirl, a pirouette, here we go,' Cohen continued.

Bouchard obliged, then giggled nervously and buried her face in her hands.

In situations like this, I like to employ the 'Would you ask Roger Federer to do a twirl?' test. Clearly the answer is 'no'.

'Touch your toes, Roge.'

'Pardon me?'

'Go on, touch your toes.'

Federer looks bemused, but being a good sport, he touches his toes.

'Love the cut of your shorts. They look like they keep your balls nice and snug.'

The men on the circuit are (mostly) spared this treatment. They're tennis players who, oddly, are asked questions about tennis. Yes, there have been some comments about the length of Pete Sampras' shorts, Roger Federer's tuxedo-style jacket and Andre Agassi's 'radical' colour choices over the years, but these episodes are few and far between compared to what women have to put up with. The twirl question and others like it don't pop up in isolation; they exist as part of the casual and entrenched sexism in sport – and society.

Only the year before, Bouchard had been faced with a similarly ridiculous question. After her win over Ana Ivanovic at the 2014 Australian Open, she was asked by former British tennis champion Samantha Smith: 'You're getting a lot of fans here, a lot of them are male, and they want to know: If you could date anyone in the world of sport, of movies – I'm sorry, they asked me to say this – who would you date?'

What is this, a world-class tennis tournament or *Perfect Match*?

At the same tournament, Maria Sharapova had to respond to an inane comment about the heat wreaking havoc on her wardrobe.

Women's tennis gets so much more media time than any other women's sport, but not without this awkward undermining of the sport itself. We need to start untangling the mess – and not only in tennis. If notorious tabloid the *Sun* can scrap its topless 'Page 3 girl', surely intelligent commentators, male and female, can lift their game.

An advantage of the cyber age is that sexist commentary gets picked up and ridiculed fast. One very effective video campaign is #CoverTheAthlete, which takes real questions and comments that have been directed at female athletes about their weight, hair and dating life, and dubs them over interviews with male athletes. 'You're getting a lot of fans here, a lot of them female, and they want to know if you could date anyone in the world, who would you date?' one asks. 'Removing your body hair gives you an edge in the pool, how about your love life?' asks another. Not surprisingly, John Inverdale's thoughts about Marion Bartoli having to compensate for her looks made the cut: in the video, a sportscaster wonders aloud whether soccer star Wayne Rooney got his drive because he doesn't look like David Beckham.

\*

Part of the problem with the sports media is that there just aren't that many women involved. Women sports journalists, like all other women in sport, put up with sexism and double standards that keep them on the outer. Sure, the number of women in our ranks is growing – when I first started as a sports journalist in 1997, it wasn't unusual for me to be the only woman at a media conference – but the atmosphere and attitudes haven't changed much.

The blokeyness of sports journalism runs deeper than

the number of women interviewing a coach: that's just the conspicuous part. Less visible are the attitudes that keep women marginalised and 'in their place'. As a woman in sport, I've been in situations where porn has been watched all around me – in the workplace, on phones, at footy training while waiting for the coach to give his doorstop interview. I never made a big deal about it because I didn't want to come across as a prude, an oversensitive moralist – despite thinking that it had no place in or around the workplace. Surely that's reasonable, like expecting employees to turn up on time and not smoke a bong at their desk.

When I read Russell Jackson's piece in the *Guardian* during the Chris Gayle controversy, it was heartening to see that I wasn't the only one in the industry uncomfortable with having to watch someone getting their porn fix:

> Last week in the Melbourne Cricket Ground press box I was staggered to note, on the third morning of the Test and for the entire day thereafter, an accredited member of the media sitting in front of me tapping away at his company laptop, but tabbing between his match report and a constant stream of hardcore pornography.
>
> I could barely believe what I was seeing. The thing that initially staggered me was the sheer audacity of it, that the presence of both female and male colleagues, who were sitting metres away with clear views of his screen, hadn't been enough to deter him, and that he felt perfectly comfortable doing it in full view. Welcome to Blokesworld.

As an industry, the Australian sports media has shared the traditions and thinking of our major games. Mostly men have been employed because, as the thinking goes, men have a better grasp and appreciation of sport. Over my career, I've heard some hilarious things directed towards me from people in positions of power and influence – well, they would have been hilarious if they weren't so career-limiting. I've been told that men don't want to hear a woman talking about sport, and that women don't want to hear a woman talking about sport either. I've been told that I'm too well spoken, too educated, a threat to the men in the office, that my 'camisole is showing too much'. And my all-time best-on-ground: 'Your side part is too pronounced.' (The man who said this looked like James Bond – if James Bond was a balding elephant seal.)

Have you ever wondered why there are so few women on radio? Because they don't sound good, so we've been told: women's voices are high-pitched and grating, not at all pleasant when you're stuck in hellish Punt Road traffic on your way to work. You need to be soothed; the last thing you need is the piercing, screechy voice of a woman coming out of your speakers – I mean, you just said goodbye to one of those forty-five minutes ago. This is the argument that commercial radio bosses use to keep their on-air talent almost exclusively male: 'Men's voices are easier on the ear.' These flimsy arguments keep men in jobs for life, limit opportunities for women and keep the status quo ticking along nicely. And the more we hear men's voices, the more conditioned we become to accept them as the norm.

Similarly, the more we hear commentators and fans complain about the noises that women tennis players make, the more we believe that these sounds are somehow more unpleasant than those that men make on court. The mere mention of Maria Sharapova sets her critics off: 'She should be banned. She sounds like she's having an orgasm.' (The chance of this being verified by any of the bleaters who say this sort of thing is about the same odds as me representing Australia in high jump at the next Olympics.)

As long as men continue to occupy the highest positions in media, cultural change will remain slow; an army of women reporters covering sport can't, by itself, wipe out negative attitudes and misconceptions about women and sport, no matter how boisterous it is. We need more women making decisions about which sports and which stories to cover.

Over the years, I've appeared on various television and radio shows discussing, both seriously and light-heartedly, sport's hot topics of the day. One thing that's struck me is that whatever the show, I was always the only woman in the line-up. I actually became used to being the sole female representative – it was just part of the deal – but it didn't stop me from thinking about how easy it would be to add another female perspective. All you'd need to do is invite another woman along. (Pleasingly, this idea looks as though it's catching on.)

A few years ago, I had an idea for an all-women AFL chat show featuring an athlete, a journalist and a comedian. When I took the idea to the networks, there was interest to develop it further, but, as an example of the way things are looked at, I was told there was one condition: if I replaced the comedian with a WAG, then I might be on to something.

In recent years, the focus of the Brownlow Medal has shifted from just the athletes to the athletes and their WAGS – with the emphasis placed squarely on looks: beauty first, woman second.

The televised red carpet entrance has become a big part of the show, and the day after the count, newspapers and websites provide verdicts on the winners and losers, complete with marks out of ten and the obligatory top three (or five or ten). Over the past two years, the Twitter campaign #AskHerMore (which began as a movement to change the questions put to women on the Hollywood red carpet) has entered the Brownlow conversation. As much as fashion is an important part of the night, some partners have added their voice to the #AskHerMore campaign, a reflection of the changing times. Nobody wants to see a repeat of 2011, with women standing on a rotating circular floor, like a carpeted microwave dish, accompanied by mean comments from the fashion police.

\*

The internet has been causing a huge cultural shift for women in sport, and the #AskHerMore social media campaign is one of many. This doesn't soothe how I feel about there being 7 per cent coverage of women's sport on traditional TV, but it does give me hope for the future.

The ASC report noted that 'by 2016–17 media distribution will be highly tailored to the customers' wants and needs', adding that 'for a larger proportion of women's sports to be commercially attractive (i.e. increasing audience), it needs to create a mass of dedicated, passionate fans' through 'a ground-up' strategy that must go beyond 'simply securing mainstream coverage'.

A wonderful example of this strategy was SBS's *Zela*, a website specifically dedicated to celebrating women's sport, where girls and women could engage in discussions about sport without being trolled, belittled or marginalised. It's sad that I have to talk about *Zela* in the past tense: it was a breath of fresh air. Its participants and creators knew how to be both serious and light-hearted, and its content was proudly and gloriously pro-woman. Most importantly, it reflected the changing landscape of Australian sport. It was, in many respects, ahead of the wave. So why did SBS pull its funding? Managing director Michael Ebeid told a Senate Estimates Committee in October 2016 that *Zela* had been shut down because it wasn't getting any traffic, something that its former editor, Danielle Warby, strongly refutes:

> Over the space of a bare 8 months Zela averaged 75,000 page views per month with a continuous upward trend … 2 days before the start of the Olympics, I was informed my contract would end at the end of the month and no more resources would be put into the site. We continued to publish already commissioned work but the wind-down had begun and an opportunity was missed to leverage the Olympics and Paralympics to grow our audience.

Warby says that the failure was in the distribution and cross-promotion of the content. When Zela's content was shared to SBS's existing, larger audiences, it did well:

> There was a lot of goodwill toward *Zela* from inside the organisation, everyone wanted it to succeed but it takes more than goodwill. A lack of strategy, structure and internal process around content management hampered the running of *Zela* and did not enable us to reach our full potential. In addition, the focus on metrics over the SBS

Charter is a dangerous path to walk and damaging to the SBS brand and mission.

It all gets back to having the will to want to change things and the patience to see them through. I often think that if decision-makers in sport afforded women the same patience that they've given to men, we'd be in a much better (and fairer) position.

A key recommendation of the ASC report was for women's sporting bodies to use its funding grants to 'create low-cost content (but high enough quality) to deliver through digital and new media platforms'. The commission's findings coincided with widespread budget cuts at the ABC, which included the axing of coverage of women's W-League soccer (later revived by a partnership between Fox Sports and ABC TV) and the Women's National Basketball League, a moment that Australian Opals superstar Lauren Jackson described as a 'very dark day for women's sport'. She's right: the national broadcaster has a responsibility to reflect social diversity, and women playing sport is part of our diverse society.

Our next generation of female basketball stars may have to turn to social media for exposure to healthy, strong women playing competitive sport. Social media gives athletes an instant connection with fans – they're able to convey messages, control how they're represented and grow a supporter base that bypasses all the biases of traditional media.

But there's a less positive side to social media, for both women athletes and women sports journalists. The widespread culture of social media trolling, without fear of consequences, means that female reporters are now subjected to vile abuse online. Digital abuse and harassment is a worldwide problem that affects everyone, but research from RMIT University (2015) found that women are twice as likely to be targeted by male offenders, and men are twice as likely to be the perpetrators of digital abuse.

To show what some women deal with, Sarah Spain and Julie DiCaro, two respected American sports journalists, featured in a powerful video titled #MoreThanMean that was controversially aimed at the average sports fan. In it, they ask a group of men to read awful, hate-filled tweets directed at the pair – and to read them out loud to their faces. The men (who aren't the original writers of the tweets) struggle with their task and apologise on behalf of the tweeters. The tweets are shocking: 'One of the players should beat you to death with their hockey stick.' 'I hope your boyfriend beats you.' 'I hope you get raped again.' 'I hope your dog gets hit by a car, you bitch.'

The late Rebecca Wilson was subjected to a tidal wave of online abuse for having strong and at times provocative opinions about sport – as is Caroline Wilson. The fact that there are men (and women) who 'like' a campaign that says, 'Share if you are against violence against women but HATE THIS HYPOCRITE' alongside a photo of Caroline Wilson, is abhorrent.

No single fix will get us to a golden age for women's sport. It will take a whole-industry approach – the sports themselves, athletes, fans, sponsors, advertisers and the media must start to believe that women's sport matters, and our words and actions must reflect this. Arguing over whether the media is or isn't the main culprit behind these years of stagnation is wasted energy. Let's forget the blame game and instead start to build up women's sport. The athletes are holding up their end of the bargain; they're breaking new ground and winning on the world stage. The rest of us must do our bit to show that women's sport is as important as men's – and one thing that we can do is to wipe out negative, unrealistic expectations of women.

# 4

---

# THE BEAUTY GAME

The Victorian woman became her ovaries, as today's woman has become her 'beauty'.

*Naomi Wolf, The Beauty Myth*

When I was in high school, friends of mine dropped out of PE because they hated the way they looked. I saw girls living on a diet of Coke, chips and cigarettes – beautiful girls who were terrified of food and already dangerously harsh on their bodies. I saw girls starving themselves to fit in, and I saw girls throwing up what they ate; I saw girls put all their energy into chasing boys and keeping up an image; I saw girls play dumb, changing their personalities to comply with someone else's sensibilities. Suddenly it was no longer okay to talk to less-fashionable types.

Because of my sport obsession, I was largely able to avoid most of this: my conquests were sports trophies. It wasn't until my late teens that I grew more interested in the whole clothes, boys, shoes and make-up thing. By that stage, my eyes had already been well and truly opened to the enormous demands imposed on teenage girls to conform with a notion of beauty pushed by glossy magazines, advertising agencies, movies and popular culture. Pushing the idea of what a woman really 'is' or 'should be' changes how we all think – even those of us who try to consciously reject those ideas.

Alarmingly, this kind of thinking has shown no sign of abating; if anything, it appears to be getting stronger. Avoiding this obsession with beauty was far easier when it wasn't coming at you from all angles, twenty-four hours a day. Teenage girls are being bombarded like never before with advertising slogans and images of celebrities, which all say that beauty is the very essence of womanhood. And because pornography is more accessible than ever, more and more women also feel pressured to live up to the expectations it creates. All over the world, girls are staring Bambi-eyed and pouty-lipped at their phones, clicking away in search of the perfect Instagram image.

In 2015, for the sixth year in a row, Mission Australia's National Youth Survey identified body image as one of the top three personal concerns for young Australians, and that concern is on the rise – from 20.4 per cent in 2012 to 26.5 per cent in 2015. Concerns about body image were considerably higher among females, with 37.4 per cent indicating that body image was a major concern, compared with 13.1 per cent of males.

Further highlighting these issues is *The Everyday Sexism* report on 'girls' and young women's views on gender inequality in Australia', commissioned by Our Watch and released on International Day of the Girl Child, 11 October 2016. Half of all girls surveyed (aged sixteen to nineteen) said that they're seldom or never valued for their brains over their looks, and only one in six said they are always valued for their brains and ability – I can't imagine only one in six boys responding the same way.

*

So how does all of this affect women in sport?

You'd think that women athletes might be immune. Sport allows girls and women to use their bodies in an active rather than a passive way – to be subjects rather than objects. Sport is about how the body is used, not how it looks. It's about physical exertion, grunt and sweat; it's about testing the body to its limits.

Unfortunately, this isn't often the way that women in sport are portrayed. Just like television shows, movies, advertisements, magazines and the internet, sport continues to push the beauty 'ideal'. Too often we see images of sportswomen as inactive, beautiful objects, and the clear message this sends is that you can only succeed in sport if you look beautiful. Equally damaging is the related message that the real reason women exercise is to make themselves look better to somebody else, rather than because it makes them feel better.

Every day, sportsmen are seen in the media doing what they do for a living – kicking a goal, taking a mark, hitting a ball, scoring a try; rarely are they seen out of context. Not only are female athletes featured in the media significantly less often than male athletes, they're also often featured for their sex appeal and not their athletic abilities – and for career survival, many women play the game.

You can easily see this play out on social media. The more followers that an athlete has, the greater their perceived worth and value; marketers and companies will often look at an athlete's social media accounts as an assessment of their popularity and potential brand reach. Followers and likes are almost as influential as gold medals when a company is determining whether to support, interview or sponsor an athlete. For sportswomen, sexy, seductive shots, with plenty of cleavage and skin, and without much focus on sport, can often get more likes and increase followers.

Jennifer Hargreaves, a prolific sport sociologist and the author of *Heroines of Sport: The Politics of Difference and Identity*, wrote this about the 'imposed heterosexuality' in female sport:

> The public image of female athletes is defined to a large degree by the media. It appears that in order to gain coverage, a woman must fit the accepted female persona. Female athletes have come to realise that they must emphasise their femininity, especially if they wish to gain sponsorship. Women who do not conform to these unwritten rules are often ridiculed and both their gender and their sexual orientation may be questioned.

The common defence by the media and sponsors is that they're just giving the audience what they want: beautiful women athletes. But they're assuming that only heterosexual men are interested in sport, followed by an assumption that the only way these men are going to be remotely interested in women's sport is if the athlete is dressed up and doing something un-athlete-like. My gut feeling is that the media and sponsors are selling men short.

Various terms have been used to describe the phenomenon of promoting sportswomen in this way, of which the most common is 'sexploitation'. Sexploitation describes forms of marketing, promotion and attempts to gain media coverage that focus attention on the sexual attributes of women athletes, especially the visibility of their bodies. Sexploitation judges the value of the woman athlete primarily in terms of her body type and attractiveness, rather than for the qualities that define her as an athlete.

In other words, sexploitation is those inane polls on television and social media sites about hot sportswomen. You can set your watch to them: the hottest tennis players in January, hottest Olympians every four years, hottest Commonwealth Games athletes every four years – all perpetuating the same two stereotypes: women exist primarily for their beauty, and men are so thick that all they care about are beautiful women. No winners here.

Remember the Women's Tennis Association's 'Strong is Beautiful' global advertising campaign? It didn't scream raging, in-your-face sexism like the Lingerie Football League did (a competition that I'll support when the Men's Netball Diamante Jockstrap League is established), but there was definitely something whiffy about it. Strangely enough, none of the campaign's images showed women tennis players doing what they actually do for a living – that is, playing tennis. I've never seen them step out onto court heavily made-up, airbrushed to within an inch of their lives and dressed in sequins. So why were these the images presented to us?

One recent example of this phenomenon caused me to stop and consider just how ingrained the sexualisation of women athletes is in our society – how far its tentacles stretch and how it can reach even the most unexpected places. The event, put on by *Women's Health* magazine, was the annual I Support Women in Sport Awards: an uplifting night that's intended to celebrate the achievements of Australia's leading women athletes by placing women firmly in the spotlight. The red carpet was awash with sporting royalty – Sally Pearson, Sally Fitzgibbons, Jessica Fox, Laura Geitz, Catherine Cox, Jordan Mercer …

… and three topless models painted as a swimmer, netballer and gymnast.

I would like to have been a fly on the wall during the meeting that came up with that idea: 'Let's celebrate our women athletes by putting them next to body-painted, half-naked models dressed up as athletes. They can mingle with the … er, real athletes on the red carpet.' Didn't *anyone* think that this might be a bit unnecessary (and insulting) to the actual athletes?

This sexualisation of women athletes is nothing new. In 'A View of the 1948 Olympics from Across the Channel: An Analysis of the French Press', Michael Attali and Jean Saint-Martin wrote about the way sportswomen were viewed at the 1948 London Games:

> Although the renewal of French sport was expected following the Liberation, media coverage during the 1948 games showed that in the French mind, it remained a bastion of masculinity – women's sport was generally ignored and/ or marked by somewhat conservative references, with the image of sportswomen being in no way equal to that of sportsmen. The officials called upon during the London games to judge the women's events were to have a rather

tricky task. Indeed, the majority of the competitors were not only sporting champions but also outstanding beauties that could have entered a cinema pin-up competition. The judges had to be scrupulously impartial and not allow themselves to be influenced by beautiful sparkling eyes that did their utmost to soften their hearts.

We know that beauty and sexiness have absolutely nothing to do with ability to play sport. In fact, there are few areas in life where they're less relevant – a particularly great outfit or 'sparkling eyes' will not give you an edge over your opponent. Yet somehow this obsession with appearance follows women athletes everywhere.

*

At the heart of this problem is the complex and troubled relationship between sport and femininity. Since we still think of sport as a masculine domain, with the 'manly' traits of strength and aggression essential for success, to be a sportswoman is to fall short of femininity – to be (shock, horror!) a woman with masculine traits. This presents a conflict for women athletes known as the 'female/athlete paradox'. Long before I knew about this term, I watched the 1992 film *A League of Their Own*, which tells the story of the inaugural season of the All-American Girls Professional Baseball League in 1940s USA. One line stood out to me back then: 'Every girl in this league is going to be a lady.'

I now understand the significance of that line. It points to the thorny problem of the woman athlete. No matter how strong, talented and powerful she is, above all else she must be a lady. The sporting and broader cultures collide and create an internal conflict. Women feel pressure to oversexualise themselves in order to prove that they're still feminine, so that they can be more popular and attract more media interest and sponsorship. Sometimes they do this by choice, on social media or otherwise, and sometimes their sport does it for them.

Jan Stephenson comes to mind, photographed naked in a bathtub full of golf balls. That was 1986. Stephenson wasn't coerced into it: she believed that the women's game needed to market its sex appeal, telling *Golf Magazine*: 'People who watch are predominantly male, and they won't keep watching if the girls aren't beautiful.' I'll take a wild stab and suggest that her comments weren't a vote-winner with those pushing for gender equality in sport.

Serena Williams's *Sports Illustrated* cover tells a similar story. The magazine's covers are generally reserved for either male athletes or female models in micro-bikinis – or, as was the case on the 2015 swimsuit edition cover, model Hannah Davis pulling down her bikini bottom. When Serena Williams was featured on the cover of the *Sports Illustrated* 'Sportsperson of the Year' issue in December 2015 (becoming the first individual woman to receive the title since Mary Decker in 1983), she chose to be photographed atop a throne, one of her legs slung over its arm, in stiletto heels, a black lace bodysuit and bare legs. In contrast, when Major League Baseball player Madison Bumgarner won 'Sportsman of the Year' in 2014, he was pictured on the cover with his San Francisco Giants gear on: glove in one hand, ball in the other, standing tall and strong. That Williams came up with her pose is a sign of how entwined sex and sport are when it comes to women – it seems that even top female athletes who've proven themselves feel the need to live up to the feminine stereotype. And we hardly blink at the sight of it.

If we were all equal, it wouldn't matter if a female athlete picked a sexy pose or got her kit off to show her fabulous body. It wouldn't be perpetuating a stereotype, and it wouldn't send the message to aspiring female athletes that it's more important to be beautiful than to be talented.

The argument often thrown at me when I criticise the sexualisation of women athletes is that male AFL players in tight shorts are sexualised too. Yes, both men and women face sexploitation, but male athletes aren't defined by their beauty in same the way as women athletes. Similarly, a calendar of buff footy players with a few strategically placed balls isn't reinforcing centuries of subordination – it's not pushing a tired old stereotype and tainting all sportsmen. Expressions of macho sexuality don't have a long history of being linked to the view that men are inferior. On top of that, the image of a manly footballer is amusing, not despite its strangeness but *because* of it. To see a footballer – that ultimate symbol of powerful manhood – exposed and vulnerable is so jarring that it's silly and can be taken as harmless fun. But when a woman poses naked, we don't find this amusing or strange because it's not 'silly': it's just something that women do.

Not everyone chooses to acknowledge the difference here. During the fallout from cricketer Chris Gayle's on-air propositioning of reporter Mel McLaughlin, perplexed sports fans drew my attention to a segment on *Sunrise* where weather presenter Nuala Hafner openly hit on a semi-naked beachgoer during a live TV segment in December 2014. Cries of 'Where was the outrage back then?' and 'Double standards!' filled the Twittersphere. Well, the thing is, you can't just pull out one example of role-reversed sexism and expect it to balance the books – that episode on the beach was a drop in the ocean (pardon the pun) compared to the endless depictions of women as passive, available flesh. And the semi-naked beachgoer wasn't just trying to do his job without being harassed. All these arguments need context.

A sportsman's societal worth has little to do with his attractiveness or sex appeal. Jason Day's worth is attached to his golf game, Tim Cahill's worth is attached to finding the back of the net, Jamie Whincup's worth is attached to his speed, and David Warner's worth is attached to his powerful batting. On the occasions when a male athlete is sexualised, he's still an athlete first, a hot dude second. We don't ask that male athletes be more or less masculine; we don't sit around and scrutinise what they're wearing; we don't demand that they smile more (as we do of Karrie Webb); and we rarely ask them to pose semi-nude to promote their sport or appease sponsors.

We don't even care much if they're single/looking for love/unlucky in love/not interested in love/a good catch/married/divorced/or a father – unless they have a hot girlfriend. Cue saturation coverage with banal references to 'batting above average' and 'punching above weight'. A hot girlfriend will inspire such remarks as that of BBC commentator Andrew Castle, who at Wimbledon in 2016 said of Marcus Willis' dental surgeon girlfriend: 'It's a pity my dentist doesn't look like that.' On its own it's a little creepy, but in the context of sport's fixation with female beauty, it carries more weight.

Just by virtue of being male, sportsmen in our major codes turn up, compete, get media coverage, get sponsorship, are hero-worshipped, become role models – and the pattern repeats itself. In some cases, it continues well into retirement, with a media gig and a comfortable cushion in a commentary box. Meanwhile, Australian sport is littered with examples of sportswomen and teams that have, either by choice or desperation, posed nude. Hockeyroo Shelley Andrews told the *Canberra Times* in 2000: 'When we take our clothes off we get more exposure than for actually playing the game.'

The question of whether it's morally right for a woman athlete to remove her clothes for a photo shoot is a tricky one. Of course, some choose this path without consciously deciding to be turned into sex objects; showing skin can be extremely empowering for some women, and it can lead to more fans and more money. It's the sporting equivalent of the Kardashian way – mass appeal creates more media interest, and that in turn creates more sponsorship opportunities. Who could blame a woman for wanting mainstream coverage, visibility, money, fame, a perfume deal and a new car?

If I abandon reality for a moment and imagine myself as an elite athlete (like I used to do as a child, holding my netball and staring up at the luminous green stars on my bedroom ceiling), and I think about the struggle that many of them face juggling work, study and sporting commitments, I admit that I'd probably get my gear off too, if it meant more support and sponsorship. (Well, ten years ago, anyway.)

But whatever their intent, women athletes who choose to do the 'sexy' photo shoots help to present themselves as 'attractive women who happen to be athletes'. And this kind of promotion has a trickle-down effect, encouraging further use of the female body as hard currency – the body's attractiveness, not its capabilities, becomes the primary selling point.

Jan Stephenson's decision to pose naked in that golf ball-filled bathtub caused a stir at the time, but when the storm died down, nothing much had changed for women's golf. Twenty years later, a new generation of female golfers was photographed nude in another attempt to generate publicity. The 2005 Women's Australian Open had been cancelled due to a lack of sponsorship and television interest, and a nude calendar was seen as a way of igniting interest in the sport. At the time one of the golfers, veteran Australian Shani Waugh, conceded: 'In an ideal world, you shouldn't have to do it.'

It's happened in soccer too. Heading into the 2000 Olympics, twelve naked Matildas were photographed for the cover of a calendar. Their motivation was to gain more media coverage and increase their public profile. While the whole team supported the calendar, there was no pressure for everyone to participate, and many of the players chose not to be included.

Perhaps the key issue here isn't so much the team's decision to market itself in this way, but that they felt it was the only way to get reasonable media coverage and sponsorship. The calendar sold out its original 35,000 print run. No matter how comfortable you are with nudity, the calendar also reinforced the message that in women's sport, sex sells. Much like in women's golf, the flurry of interest didn't achieve anything at the time. Today, the Matildas are arguably the most compelling national team in the country – nothing beats on-field success. I'd also argue that the strength shown by the players in their campaign for better pay and conditions has added another layer of admiration and respect.

The Matildas' 2000 nude calendar had flow-on effects for other sports. In April of that year, the national women's netball team also decided to produce a calendar to raise funds and awareness – not a nude calendar, though. When the players turned up for the photo shoot, photographers pressured them to take their clothes off. In the end, the team ruled decisively that posing nude wasn't the way they wanted their family-friendly sport to be depicted in a calendar. In the *Age* article 'Taking a Stand for Skill over Skin', Australian defender Janine Ilitch presented the players' case: 'I think for female sports to be taken seriously, we should be recognised for our skills and achievements rather than our naked bodies.' Vice-captain Liz Ellis raised another risk of sexploitation: 'I'm also a solicitor, and I couldn't imagine going into a conference with a client and for them to have looked at me that morning on their son's bedroom wall, nude or semi-nude.'

But plenty of high-profile Australian sportswomen have exploited their sex appeal at the peak of their careers – heptathlete Jane Flemming opted for gold paint and nothing else on the cover of the 'Golden Girls' calendar in 1995; Hockeyroo Louise Dobson posed naked, her back to the camera, next to a pear to help out the Shepparton fruit industry; pole-vaulter Tatiana Grigorieva went full-frontal for *Black & White* magazine in 2000; Opals basketballer Lauren Jackson graced the cover of *Black & White's The Athens Dream* in 2004, her long, blonde hair-extensions strategically placed to cover her nipples; and others, including runner Tamsyn Lewis, have posed for *Ralph*. Is it a coincidence that these photographs have been taken in Olympic years? For every athlete who wants to pose nude, there's one who feels compromised into doing it to cover basic expenses for training, equipment and travel.

The link between beauty and sponsorship for women in sport is as clear as the nose on your face. In 2013, Ellyse Perry appeared on the front cover of the *Sunday Telegraph*'s 'Body + Soul' lift-out, under the headline 'Meet Australia's most marketable athlete'. Perry had just signed a deal with underwear giant Jockey; in celebration of this, she was photographed in underwear and a hoodie unzipped to her waist. Perry is an enormously talented athlete who's represented Australia in two sports: cricket and soccer. She also fits the mould of what's conventionally attractive by Western standards – blonde, blue-eyed and slim. She is, to use the vernacular, a 'sponsor's dream'. This is magnificent for Perry. She is grounded and pragmatic and deserves every opportunity that comes her way. She knows that most sponsorship money goes to male athletes because they're more visible, and what's left goes to those sportswomen deemed feminine enough. She knows that she's one of the lucky ones. In an interview with *Mamamia*, she acknowledged this: 'It's not just about [women's] athletic ability, it's about how marketable they are from an aesthetic point of view. This doesn't happen as much in male sport because they're in the public eye a lot more.'

It's hardly surprising that eight of the world's top ten highest-paid female athletes of 2016 were tennis players: Serena Williams (1), Maria Sharapova (2), Agnieszka Radwanska (5), Caroline Wozniacki (6), Garbine Muguruza (7), Ana Ivanovic (8), Victoria Azarenka (9), and Eugenie Bouchard (10). Retired

Russian tennis player Anna Kournikova's net worth is estimated at $50 million, despite her never winning a WTA singles tournament: her overall prize money is approximately $3.5 million. These women are all wonderful athletes, but on top of that they play a sport that oozes femininity – from the clothes the players wear and the media's preoccupation with them (sometimes fuelled by the players themselves) to the boring and predictable questions about their private lives (that is, of course, if they're heterosexual).

Mixed martial artist Ronda Rousey came in at number three on the Forbes list and NASCAR driver Danica Patrick at four. Both women are beautiful and have been comfortable posing in minimal clothing or a coat of paint to promote themselves and their sport.

Sportswomen have fought hard for the incremental gains that have been made over many years, and they've fought hard for whatever media coverage they can get that doesn't focus on superficial issues. The danger of athletes saying 'yes' to sexploitation is that it sends conflicting and confusing messages to the media, the community and other athletes – on the one hand, we want to be taken seriously as athletes; on the other, we're happy to be presented as a pretty, sexy package. This can help to undermine all the good work that women in sport have done to be taken seriously. It may be seen as culturally inappropriate or sexist; it may make girls and women feel more self-conscious about their bodies, and alienate LGBTI+ people because it only promotes a stereotypical heterosexual image.

*

Reinforcing appearance over talent can also affect the self-esteem of female athletes. These women have heightened body awareness; in younger athletes, where self-confidence may be lacking, the increased focus on the body through sexploitation can create serious issues.

Flick through Leisel Jones's 2015 memoir, *Body Lengths*, and you'll see very clearly the link between elite sport and body image problems. Jones won nine Olympic medals over four Games. In *Body Lengths*, she tells of how difficult it was growing up in a pair of bathers in the public eye – and the impact that this had on her mental health. She describes how she came to find herself sitting on the bathroom floor of a hotel in Spain one afternoon in 2011, with a box of sleeping tablets and a plan to kill herself.

Jones also says that she was 'actively encouraged' to skip meals, and at the Queensland Academy of Sport the swimmers were weighed three times a week. Girls bore the brunt of this.

Weigh-ins take place on the pool deck in our togs, and we are weighed in front of our squad (girls and guys together), plus a team of coaching staff. There are men there as old as our dads, all watching our embarrassment as we are publicly weighed.

Weighed, weighed and weighed again.

Some of the coaches at the QAS gym have a thing going called '6:1.20'. This is their code, their secret talk. They think we don't understand when they call a girl – it's always a girl – a '6:1:20'. But when she's crying in the showers later, it's because she knows that '6' stands for the sixth letter of the alphabet, '1' the first, and '20' the twentieth. F. A. T. Doesn't take a genius to bust that one open.

Athletes spend every day thinking about their bodies – after all, their bodies are their way of earning money and success. But in women, that pressure goes beyond the body's suitability for its sport, because there's pressure for that body to be aesthetically perfect too.

Jones's coaches may have thought that they were just doing what needed to be done to get the best out of their swimmers, but then why did girls bear the brunt of it? Why did that secret code apply only to girls?

I'd suggest that it's because policing, judging and criticising women's bodies is second nature. Jones couldn't just swim well, she had to look the part too. Like most girls, Jones had an image in her head of what she should have looked like, and she couldn't live up to it. She was convinced that she was fat. An arbitrary (and cruel) measurement of her body became the only thing that mattered. It sucked the joy out of her sport and became her obsession.

*

To participate in some sports, you need to wear revealing clothes. Track and field athletes of both sexes wear body-hugging outfits designed to let them go faster and higher with the least restriction and wind resistance, while swimming has long meant tight costumes.

Women's beach volleyball, on the other hand, introduced uniforms in order to focus attention on women's bodies rather than for any technological, practical or performance-enhancing reasons. In the lead-up to the 2000 Sydney Olympics, the International Volleyball Federation introduced a rule that female players had to wear bikinis that were no more than six centimetres wide at the hip (men could continue to compete in shorts and singlets). The CEO of Volleyball Australia, Craig Carracher, backed the worldwide decision, saying: 'If we can show off these bodies at the same time as presenting our sport then we are going to do that.' Thirteen years after that edict, the sport's ruling body backed down, conceding that its rules were discouraging some women from playing the sport and were a barrier to the expansion of beach volleyball in conservative countries. At the 2012 London Olympics, women were allowed to compete in shorts and sleeved tops.

That same year, the Australian Opals basketballers ditched their skin-tight bodysuits in favour of looser clothing after the players lobbied for change.

Here's a stranger example: in 2010, the governing body of boxing, the International Boxing Association (AIBA), began handing out skirts to its female fighters. Its president, Wu Ching-kuo, said that audiences couldn't tell the difference between the men and the women, especially on TV. The mandate to wear skirts never went through, but wearing skirts is still an option – one with very little appeal for women boxers.

Surfing, in contrast, is one of those sports in which the costume needs to be skin-tight. But just how revealing? In July 2013, Roxy, one of women's surfing's major sponsors, released a video featuring five-time world champion Stephanie Gilmore's morning routine. They filmed her half-naked, tanned legs wrapped around bedsheets and her shoulders in the shower before following her in short-shorts on a journey to the beach. We don't see any clips of her surfing, but by the time it finishes we know every square centimetre of her bum.

The backlash to this trailer was swift and savage. Worldwide surf journalist Ted Endo had this blunt message for Roxy: 'Why can't you just say, "Yeah we fucked up." We took one of the finest athletes the world has ever seen and made a video clip of her butt because we thought it would get attention.' He went on to make the point that people 'really just want to see women portrayed as more than just a sum of their overly sexualised parts'.

Then, in March 2014, thirteen-year-old surfer Olive Bowers wrote a strong letter to the editor of Australian surf magazine *Tracks*:

Dear Tracks Surf Magazine,

I want to bluntly address the way you represent women in your magazine. I am a surfer, my dad surfs and my brother has just started surfing.

Reading a *Tracks* magazine I found at my friend's holiday house, the only photo of a woman I could find was 'Girl of the month'. She wasn't surfing or even remotely near a beach. Since then I have seen some footage of Stephanie Gilmore surfing on your website, but that's barely a start.

I clicked on your web page titled 'Girls' hoping I might find some women surfers and what they were up to, but it entered into pages and pages of semi-naked, non-surfing girls.

These images create a culture in which boys, men and even girls reading your magazine will think that all girls are valued for is their appearance.

My posse of female surfers and I are going to spread the word and refuse to purchase or promote *Tracks* magazine. It's a shame that you can't see the benefits of an inclusive surf culture that in fact, would add a whole lot of numbers to your subscription list.

I urge you to give much more coverage to the exciting women surfers out there, not just scantily clad women (who may be great on the waves, but we'll never know).

I would subscribe to your magazine if only I felt that women were valued as athletes instead of dolls.

This change would only bring good.

Olive

The letter went viral, reaching women who are generally fed up with sexism as well as women who surf.

The furore surrounding the sport even inspired a PhD on women's surfing and sponsorship in 2015. Southern Cross University academic Dr Roslyn Franklin's research showed that sport fans were more interested in seeing women surfers in action. Despite this, she found that the industry continued to sexualise them, which contributed to them not being taken seriously: 'When you look at how men are portrayed and women are portrayed, particularly in magazines and on websites, usually the men are portrayed in the act of doing the sporting performance and the women are shown in their bikinis or a view from behind.'

Speaking of views from behind: the Lingerie Football League (rebranded as the Legends Football League) landed in Australia in 2013 with four teams: the New South Wales Surge,

Queensland Brigade, Victoria Maidens and Western Australia Angels. For those who missed it, it was women's gridiron with a twist – that twist being the bit about lingerie.

'It sounds great, Bob, I mean, I'm all for the ladies having a chance to show off their stuff, I mean some of these gals, very impressive, but ... I dunno, the outfit, will we be able to see any, um ... breasts?'

'Look, don't panic, you'll be able to see the outlines, sort of –'

'Wouldn't it make sense to maybe get rid of the top altogether and just have them in their ... y'know, bras?'

'Steve, you're a genius!'

'We could call it the Brassiere Football League.'

'It certainly sounds classy ...'

In an insult to long-standing women's sports, the LFL secured a national free-to-air television contract with the Seven Network's 7 Mate in its inaugural season. And I'm sure that this had nothing to do with boobs and butt. Nothing at all.

But with less than two weeks before the scheduled kick-off for 2014–15, the season was cancelled amid controversy involving two class-action lawsuits. The Seven Network pulled out as host broadcaster after one season. In February 2015, players and coaches left and joined the Ladies Gridiron League – with a uniform change.

*

The way forward for women in sport is to put athletes first. Before sex and beauty.

When this happens, even nudity doesn't have to be sexploitation. Instead of cutting it out completely, it might be best to support more publications like *ESPN Magazine*'s 'Body Issue', which features nude female and male athletes, and depicts women athletes of all body types (including Paralympians) in generally active poses. This treatment of sportswomen, which praises their athleticism and the hard work that it takes to shape their bodies, is a huge breath of fresh air compared to the content of magazines like *Sports Illustrated*.

Girls and women shouldn't have to choose between sport and femininity. They should be able to express who they are through their sport. For this to occur, women must continue to challenge the status quo by participating more frequently in more varieties of sport. Only then can we successfully redefine what it means to be a sportswoman in Western culture – and only then will the kneejerk response to promote beauty before athleticism disappear.

# 5

## INVISIBILITY

The return of Australian Rules football to Adelaide Oval was a glorious moment for all of us who have South Australian blood coursing through our veins. From my adopted home of Melbourne, I watched the hoopla of the first Showdown at Adelaide Oval in 2014. I was aching to be there – my old hometown was shining, and I missed her terribly on that Saturday. The redevelopment of the ground was a victory for perseverance and for all sports fans in a town hamstrung by tensions between cricket and Australian Rules since the 1960s.

But despite all the excitement, I couldn't shake a nagging, uneasy feeling. I'm not talking about the one I get before every Showdown – this was something quite different.

A few days before the historic match, I'd read about Barrie Robran becoming the first football great honoured with a bronze statue at Adelaide Oval. *Terrific*, I thought. *You can't argue with three Magarey Medals.* He's one of four football icons to be recognised in this way at the revamped oval; the others are

Russell Ebert, Ken Farmer and Malcolm Blight. Statues have also been commissioned to honour four South Australian cricketers – Darren Lehmann, Jason Gillespie, George Giffen and Clem Hill. Max Basheer, the SANFL's longest-serving president and the man responsible for the creation of Football Park, is one of five men with a pavilion named after him in the Eastern Stand; the others are Gavin Wanganeen, Jack Oatey, Fos Williams and Mark Ricciuto. The Chappell Stand recognises brothers Ian, Greg and Trevor. There's also the Bob Quinn Gate, adjacent to the Clarrie Grimmett Gate, the William Magarey Room, the Graham Cornes Deck, the Rick Davies Stadium Club Bar, the Neil Kerley Members' Bar and the Lindsay Head Terrace. The names Bob Hank and Len Fitzgerald adorn the two bridges that link the Southern and Eastern stands, while John Cahill and Andrew McLeod have a room each in the Southern Stand, a stab pass from the Peter Carey Bar. Are you detecting a trend? The John Halbert Room is located in the Eastern Stand with a section for the John Platten Bar, and on the ground level is the Garry McIntosh Bar. And there's the Leigh Whicker League Room too.

I'm surprised they didn't commission a giant set of brass testicles to hang above the entrance.

This is in the same state that gave women the vote before all others, in 1894. (Interestingly, suffragette Mary Lee and other significant women used the ladies' room at the Adelaide Oval for meetings in the lead-up to the vote.)

But let's stick with cricket. Where's the recognition of the talented women cricketers who have represented South Australia and our country? For a state with such a proud record of achievements by women – sporting and otherwise – this is a disgrace. Are you seriously telling me that a half a billion-dollar redevelopment couldn't find one woman worthy of a blade of grass named after her? Karen Rolton captained Australia! *CAPTAINED*. She retired as Australia's highest run-scorer in Test cricket and was named Australian women's player of the year a record four times. Throw in a test average of 55.66 and 209 not out against England at Headingley, and you have a powerful case for recognition – the Rolton Stand has a good ring to it. And here are a few others that the eight men who make up the Adelaide Oval Stadium Management Authority should have considered: Lyn 'Lefty' Fullston, Joanne Broadbent and Jill Kennare – all trailblazers in cricket. All thoroughly deserving. What about Faith Thomas, who in 1958 became the first Indigenous person selected to play cricket for their country and the first Indigenous woman selected to play *any* sport for Australia?

South Australian football great Graham Cornes said that it would be 'tokenism at its most blatant' to honour South Australian women cricketers at Adelaide Oval. Graham, you're missing the point. This is about equality. This is about inspiring girls to fulfil their dreams. This is about girls walking through Adelaide Oval and seeing a reflection of themselves on the walls, terraces and honour boards. It's about a sense of belonging that empowers girls with the belief that one day they too could be cast in bronze.

A year and a half after I raised this glaring oversight, the SACA announced the creation of the Lyn Fullston Lawns between the new Riverbank and Western grandstands and the indoor training centre. It will serve as a place of reflection and a memorial to the popular player and coach who lost her battle with cancer in 2008 at the age of fifty-two. Lyn 'Lefty'

Fullston was a multi-talented sportswoman and teacher who represented Australia in cricket and netball. After a fifteen-year career, she retired as the only female Australian cricketer to take 100 international wickets. A special women's hall of fame area – featuring South Australian and Australian cricketers Karen Rolton, Shelley Nitschke, Faith Thomas and Joanne Broadbent – was also unveiled at the oval.

The SACA should be applauded for finally recognising these women, but it should have been done at the grand opening of the new Adelaide Oval in February 2014. This big occasion was a missed opportunity to send a powerful symbolic message about the value of women athletes and women's sport. Our girls deserved better.

\*

Any woman who breaks down boundaries in male-dominated areas has a story to tell, and we need to hear these stories. We can learn so much from them about leadership, adversity, strength and humour. Seeing a reflection of ourselves is empowering and motivating, and makes it a whole lot easier to visualise a clear pathway, rather than one full of potholes and ill-informed attitudes.

In the heavily masculine world of sport, role models are especially important for women and girls, because encouragement in the form of a role model can be the difference between a girl staying in a sport and her giving it up. Studies have shown that girls as young as nine can become self-conscious about their bodies; exposing girls to successful, confident, strong athletic female role models with a healthy variety of body shapes gives them positive images to look up to: the kind that society is crying out for.

Sport is built on the role of the hero, and even though the rose-tinted glasses I wore as a teenager have been replaced with plain contact lenses, I still think that sport is littered with genuine heroes. That's always been a big part of its attraction for me. What makes the game so great? The thrill of playing it, of course, but also the thrill of seeing it played at its very, very best – by a sports star at the peak of their powers, doing the seemingly impossible.

As a young girl, my pool of sporting role models was a shallow one. Not because there weren't any talented and inspiring sportswomen out there – there were – but they were largely invisible. Usually they only came out of the shadows at tennis majors (I grew up in the era of Martina Navratilova and Chris Evert). Every four years, I'd perch in front of the television to watch the Olympics or the Winter Olympics, where I'd be reminded that women compete in more than just tennis.

As a ten-year-old, I wasn't aware of the media's power – all I knew was that I loved sport. So, like the other sports-mad girls I knew, I latched on to male sporting role models. When I flew for a mark, I was Norwood great Roger Woodcock. When I spun out of a pack and snapped a goal, I was Michael Aish. When I pretended to be tough, I was Craig Balme in the goal square punching on with Tim Evans during the national anthem at the 1984 SANFL Grand Final. I kept a Kim Hughes scrapbook and modelled my own dancing-down-the-wicket batting technique on his. I always had to be a man – we all did. And in the back of our minds, it just hammered in the idea that 'serious' sport was only for boys and men.

If, however, there was a scandal of some kind, women athletes would receive the same amount of coverage as a male athlete in the prime of his non-controversial career. Nancy Kerrigan v Tonya Harding; Mary Decker v Zola Budd – I can still remember where I was sitting in the lounge room and what I was wearing (not hard, I suppose, when you have a tracksuit for every day of the week) when Budd accidentally tangled with Decker, causing her to fall in the 3000-metres final at the 1984 Los Angeles Games. With so little coverage of women's sport outside of the Olympics, this was big news in my world and the world at large.

Closer to home, role models were even harder to find. My parents gave me a book about Evonne Goolagong Cawley for my fifteenth birthday. I kept it close to me that summer, and by the time the new season came along, I'd almost memorised it. In between cricket matches, I'd read and re-read passages, and in the evenings after dinner I'd draw my family in close, take centre stage in the lounge room, and read my favourite parts out loud. I wasn't making a political statement about women being forgotten in Australian history – that realisation would come a few years later – I just felt connected to her story.

Imagine if the stories of sportswomen were told as often as men's. What would that do to the value we place on women athletes? Historian Clare Wright observes: 'Women's history can lead us back to familiar terrains and refract "the truth" in a different light.' Maybe a look back in time, through the eyes of Australia's sportswomen, would help those who undervalue their current achievements to see things differently.

*

To fill the gaps in my Australian sporting history, I read books and articles, and that's how I discovered Betty Wilson – the sportswoman who should be just as much of an inspiration to all Australians as Sir Donald Bradman has been.

Wilson was named in the *2014 Wisden Cricketers' Almanack* as one of its five greatest female cricketers of all time, along with two other Australians, Belinda Clark and Cathryn Fitzpatrick, as well as England's Enid Bakewell and India's Mithali Raj. We should all know Wilson's story – it should be celebrated and passed down like Bradman's story, Keith Miller's story, Richie Benaud's story – but we don't, because women's cricket lives in the shadow of men's cricket, as is customary for most sports.

Also hidden is the vibrant history of women's cricket in Australia, which dates back to the late nineteenth century. Founding mother Lily Poulett-Harris, a Tasmanian, captained the Oyster Cove Ladies Cricket Club in the league she created in 1894. By the following year, the ladies' competition was turning heads, as noted by a sports journalist in the *Mercury* on 2 December 1895: '(Interest in cricket) seems to be growing, and extending to the weaker sex, who often have a quiet match upon a romantic little plateau on the Domain immediately beyond the upper cricket ground.'

Funnily enough, some members of the 'weaker sex' became very good at cricket. Betty Wilson practised her game by hitting a ball stuffed in one of her mother's stockings suspended from a clothesline. Her skills were so good that she was persuaded to join the Collingwood Women's Cricket Club in Melbourne in 1932. Wearing a borrowed dress that had been specially shortened by one of the players, she made her debut at the age of ten. At fourteen she was in the Victorian 2nd XI, and at sixteen she was in the firsts.

Wilson had to wait until after World War II to play Test cricket for Australia, but when the moment arrived, she dazzled in her debut against New Zealand, scoring 90 and taking 4 for 37 and 6 for 28. In her second Test, she became the first Australian woman to score a century against England (and there were nine more wickets). During the 1950s, Wilson was nicknamed the female Bradman. In 1958, playing against England in Melbourne, she became not only the first woman player but also the first player in the game to take ten wickets – her figures were 11 for 16 – and to score a century in the same Test.

In an era when women cricketers trained once a week, Wilson trained every day. She never married; her fiancé twice agreed to postpone their wedding because of cricket commitments, but when Wilson decided to tour England in 1951 it was the end of the relationship. There was no contraceptive pill in those days, so Wilson turned convention on its head and chose cricket over becoming a wife and mother. 'It depended what you wanted out of life,' she told the National Library of Australia. 'Who was going to knock a chance to go to England and play cricket? No. No way.'

In 2007, I was lucky enough to meet Wilson on day two of the Boxing Day Test in Melbourne. We shared the stage at the MCC Women in Cricket Test Breakfast – and she had the crowd in stitches. When I quizzed her about why she never married, she quipped: 'Righto you men, all leave the room! What I'd say in female company I'm not prepared to say here. But there's a little white thing that ladies take nowadays that makes it different altogether.'

Wilson's love of the game filled the room – we all left feeling privileged to have met such a remarkable woman and cricketer; we all left feeling better about the sport we love.

Betty Wilson should be a revered Australian and a role model to generations of girls, but she's not, because we celebrate the achievements of sportsmen above sportswomen. We praise, glorify and eulogise men who accomplish less than women. We blindly follow the minutiae of our favourite footy players, while ignoring the successes of women athletes on the world stage.

In the lead-up to the 2016 federal election, Labor promised $21 million over four years to the ABC to increase its coverage of women's sport by five hundred live hours across television and digital platforms. But when Labor leader Bill Shorten was asked to name the captains of the Hockeyroos, the Diamonds and the Southern Stars, he could only come up with Laura Geitz from netball and the surname of the Southern Stars captain. I'm not questioning how passionate Shorten is about women's rights, sport and equality, but his forgetfulness points to the problem that many of these women fly under the radar.

We gather around and applaud the unveiling of every new bronze statue of a man outside a sports stadium, but rarely question where the women are. Where's the bronze statue of Wilson? There isn't one. Even in 2006, when Wilson became the first Australian woman to be granted honorary membership of the Melbourne Cricket Club, the headline in Geoff McLure's *Sporting Life* column was 'Now it's Slater HCM': Michael Slater, Saeed Anwar, Andy Flower and Courtney Walsh were also honoured that year. This was a missed opportunity to make a splash about Wilson.

*

There have been many missed opportunities for the media to acknowledge women's successes, and this is partly why female sporting role models are hard to find. We already know that the media supports and perpetuates stereotypes that keep athletes like Wilson unknown; it makes decisions based on the assumption that sport is predominantly played by men for men, keeping men front and centre and women on the fringes.

But this isn't just the media's fault. We're all guilty of acting as though men's sport is more important than women's sport and, oh well, that's just the way it is. We turn up in droves to watch men's sport; we hear comments denigrating women's sport and do nothing about it; we don't make the effort to know the captains of our major national women's teams, but we can name most players who line up in our men's teams; we watch and listen to all-male panels and commentary teams and do nothing about it; and we refuse to talk about women's sport as a women's rights issue. Apathy stands in the way of women athletes being better known to us all.

When I was sixteen, I was invited to train with Garville A1s Netball Club in Adelaide. During a training session a few years later, I saw Michelle den Dekker, who'd come across from a rival club to lead the A1s. I'd often seen her at netball on Saturdays, and I knew that she was from the same part of Adelaide as me. This gave me an instant connection to her, even though physically we're from different planets – den Dekker was a tall and powerful defender, the best I've ever seen play the game, while I was built for the midcourt, not so tall and not as powerful. Watching her train on the court next to mine was as close as I'd got to netball royalty. She was mentally tough and driven to succeed – I thought that if I trained harder and practised my drills at home, I'd soon be on the same court as her on those crisp Tuesday evenings in Adelaide's netball-nuts north-eastern suburbs. When I went home that evening, I told my mum all about being so close to den Dekker, one court away.

While den Dekker was a legend in netballing circles, she was by no means a household name like the local footballers, whose names and photos appeared everywhere – newspapers, collection cards, cereal boxes and on TV. Like the boys I hung out with, I idolised a few of the Norwood footballers and talked as though I had a personal connection to them. But whenever I brought up den Dekker and tried to convince the boys that she was equally amazing, they just didn't get it: 'She can't really be that big of a deal because we haven't heard of her.' 'She's only a netballer, Ange ...'

Michelle den Dekker would go on to win world championships, Commonwealth Games gold and become Australia's longest-serving netball captain. She was my sporting role model – but like so many women athletes of my generation, she was unheard of and undervalued outside her chosen sport. We know that there's a link between this kind of invisibility and the participation rate of girls in organised sport. It's so much easier to aspire to be the best when you have a vision of the best in front of you, talking directly to you.

Unfortunately, many of the women paid to be associated with sport aren't sporting role models. They're something else entirely.

# 6

---

# GARNISH

Most progressive restaurants and home chefs have phased out the old way of thinking that no dish, no matter how complex and delicious, is complete without the addition of a single sprig of parsley – the same sprig that's left at the end of the meal, stranded on the outer lip of the dish after being shunted as far from the food (and fork) as is physically possible within the confines of its 360-degree perimeter. It's difficult to pinpoint exactly when the realisation dawned that despite its appealing greenness and not wholly unpleasant taste, parsley is about as effective as racing stripes on a Toyota Corona.

Surely it's also time for us to rethink the way that we use women as garnish during sporting events? It seems there's an unwritten rule stipulating that in order for an event to succeed as a spectacle, attractive women must be standing by the sportsmen – literally standing beside them in bikinis, short-shorts, short skirts, lycra or national dress.

Or, in the case of Formula One, dressed immaculately (in

matching trim) and standing in an obedient line to applaud the exclusively male drivers at the end of every race. All that's missing is a curtsey. Meanwhile, the podium girls at the Tour de France wear polka dots for mountain climbs, yellow dresses for overall title contenders, or a serious shade of salmon pink (as is also the custom at Adelaide's Tour Down Under). Their job is to dutifully hand out flowers or teddies or wine or chocolates, and a kiss to the sweaty cheek of the winner of each stage.

Even in my sister's house, where my teenage nephews have been protected from the evils of feminism, eyebrows were raised in unison at the end of the Tour Down Under this year: 'Why are those women there?' I tried to explain just how precarious the climb up onto the podium can be in 35-degree heat – more dangerous than the Col du Tourmalet in the Pyrenees, especially in those clip-clopping shoes – but this didn't wash with my nephews. Seriously, is 'just being there' (albeit while wearing a smile) a good look in this day and age? I would argue that using women as decorative objects sends an unequivocal message about the way that certain sports view women.

Motor sport, cycling, boxing, mixed martial arts, darts, football and basketball all use a variation of the podium girl – women as appendages to men – and that makes them either a much-loved and integral part of male sport or a sexist anachronism. Or, for some people, both.

Sexualising female athletes diminishes the perception of their talent and makes it harder for them to be taken seriously, and it also pushes girls away from sport. Having women as garnish is even worse, because it basically shouts: 'Sport is for men, and the only way we need women involved is as cute little decorations.'

*

The most visible of these 'girls' are in Formula One and the Tour de France. F1 has a global TV audience of half a billion, and Le Tour at least 3.5 billion. These events are all about sponsorship, and the podium girl concept is based on the belief that sex sells.

Back in 1950s Las Vegas, when ring girls were introduced to promote boxing fights, the 'sex sells' idea wasn't so out of step with the rest of society. Men and women had more clearly defined roles: in Australia, most people got married in their early twenties, and it wasn't unusual for a woman to give up her job when she got married, or at least when she had her first child. Men were the earners and made the household purchasing decisions (with the exception of groceries). Because sponsors were selling to a primarily male audience, sexualised women were a sure-fire way to get their attention.

Most Westerners would agree that things have changed since the fifties – well, in most places. UK journalist Beverley Turner was a member of ITV's F1 coverage team for three years in the early 2000s. In her 2004 book, *The Pits: The Real World of Formula One*, she rips into the sport's culture – the greed, the smoke and mirrors and the blatant sexism: 'I felt trapped in this world of horrible rich small men, and there was no escape.' On the subject of grid girls, here's what she had to say about the Australian F1 Grand Prix:

[It] boasts the highest percentage of bare flesh per driver. Promotional models walk the circuit handing out leaflets and posing for photos with punters. They move around in groups, huddling together ever more closely as drunken men hug their bare shoulders and slobber kisses on their cheeks.

Make no mistake, glamour on the grid is an edict from the top. A letter from F1 chief Bernie Ecclestone in May 2013 to then-Caterham team principal Cyril Abiteboul about the issuing of grid passes spells it out in no uncertain terms:

Dear Cyril

Please be reminded that where possible, grid access passes should be used for celebrities or people of note or as always, really glamorous ladies.

This is not so much a sporting matter but part of the show business of Formula One.

Best wishes

Bernie

This tradition embodies two assumptions: that women exist only for the gratification of men, and that motor racing needs the allure of glamorous women to attract fans. The first is clearly wrong – and every time that kind of thinking rears its head, it should be called out in the strongest possible terms. The second sells the sport and its fans short.

You don't need a double degree in feminist theory to draw a link between women being treated as garnish and the reinforcement of a sense of entitlement among men. This is perhaps best encapsulated by Lewis Hamilton champagne-spraying a grimacing podium girl after the 2015 Chinese Grand Prix, an act that drew worldwide condemnation.

Promotional models at sporting events are there to serve men, and this feels hopelessly out of step with our changing society – fortunately, the head of the Australian F1 Grand Prix, Andrew Westacott, recognises this. Just after announcing a new partnership with White Ribbon Australia in 2016, he conceded that grid girls are an outdated concept. But he stopped short of saying that the practice should be abandoned, suggesting instead that 'the day of the stereotypical view of the grid girl is numbered'. Perhaps the association with White Ribbon will provoke some serious debate around the boardroom table. White Ribbon encourages men to stand up, speak out and act 'to end men's violence against women and girls, promote gender equality, healthy relationships and a new vision of masculinity'. Eighty per cent of F1's target audience is men, so the alliance could potentially make a real difference.

This is where sport is at its best – when it's connected to something much greater than itself. Nonetheless, thanks to the prominence of promotional girls and the lack of visible female race drivers in F1, the message coming out of the sport remains that it's a man's game. On the matter of women drivers, Westacott says don't hold your breath: 'The evidence would suggest it's going to be a fair while.'

As a nation, we're still learning about the damaging effects of sexist attitudes. New research shows that young people are struggling to work out what healthy, respectful relationships look like. A 2015 survey of over three thousand young men and women commissioned by *Our Watch* found that one in six 12- to 24-year-olds believe that 'women should know their place'; one in three young people don't think that exerting control over someone else is a form of violence; one in four don't think that it's serious when guys insult or verbally harass girls in the street; one in four think it's pretty normal for guys to pressure girls into sex; and more than a quarter think that it's important for men to be tough and strong. Such attitudes give rise to discrimination and violence.

Against this backdrop, and the ongoing fight for equality and respect in sport, it seems incongruous that women are paraded at the F1 as decorative pieces – to serve men and add glamour.

While F1 has been slow to act, the winds of change are sweeping through other categories of motorsport. The World Endurance Championship scrapped the grid girl altogether at the start of the 2015 season. At the time, series CEO Gerard Neveu said, 'It's old-school to have such a concept as grid girls. Surely the world's moved on? And motor racing should follow quite closely what the rest of the world's doing in that respect … the star at the end is the sports cars and the drivers of the car.'

At the 2016 Clipsal 500 in Adelaide, it came to light that the South Australian government is planning to scrap taxpayer funding of promotional models at the V8 Supercars event that it owns. Tourism minister Leon Bignell explained the decision: 'I think it's not a good spend of taxpayers' money when we're putting money in one area of government to help young women [with body image problems] and in another area we're paying for other young women to dress up in skimpy outfits.'

Grid girls in F1 may not dress as provocatively as in other categories of racing, but that's not the point – it's not about the cut, shape or quality of the fabric. In 2016, the F1 grid girls were more flight attendant than exotic dancer, but they were still pure garnish.

*

Cycling is also steeped in a very macho culture, and it's taken many years for women's cycling to build a strong following and get even a smidgen of the respect that it deserves. Tales of sexism and sexist attitudes are rife in the cycling world – and you could hardly say that those responsible for them are being discouraged.

Consider the marketing campaign (clearly inspired by the TV show *Mad Men*) for the 2015 Belgian road-cycling classic E3 Harelbeke, which features a cyclist's hand homing in on the shapely, uncovered bottom of a podium girl – uncovered because her skirt has been thrown up by a very focused gust of wind – with a tagline that reads: 'Who squeezes them in Harelbeke?'

This campaign paid homage to Peter Sagan (nicknamed 'The Terminator'), a Slovakian rider who pinched the bottom of a podium girl as she was kissing the cheek of Fabian Cancellara at the Tour of Flanders in 2013. Matt Rendell, the press chief for cycling's Movistar team, tweeted at the time: 'Sagan's carefully thought-out piece of theatrical satire brilliantly focused attention on the absurdity of still having podium girls in 2013.' But Sagan's defenders didn't bring political statement into the mix – they relied more on pleas to consider the cyclist's youth and talent before condemning him. In response, Jane Aubrey, editor of Australian *Cycling News*, tweeted: 'Anyone excusing Sagan's behaviour due to his age needs to think again. In the workplace, it's called harassment.'

Sagan later took to Twitter to apologise: 'Was not my intention to disrespect women today on the podium. Just a joke, sorry if someone was disturbed about it.' Another 'joke' to add to the pile of harmless jokes that use women as their punchline: apparently the default position for men in sport who are attempting to be funny. There was an air of familiarity about the qualified apology too – not just in using the 'joke' as a get-out-of-jail-free card, but also in using the word 'if'.

The organisers of the 2015 Flanders Diamond Tour (the penultimate stage of the Lotto Cycling Cup) took absurdity to a whole new level. After the stage from Antwerp to Nijlen, the winners of the women's road race were greeted by four women wearing the tiniest of black bikinis; they stood at the base of the podium, two on either side. The stage was won by Jolien d'Hoore in her first race back from a six-week layoff, but her victory was overshadowed by yet another demeaning display – this one centre-stage at a women's event. Who in their right mind thought that it was okay to have four models in skimpy bikinis stand in front of a group of elite sportswomen? Borat, perhaps? The Lotto Cycling Cup issued an apology after cycling journalist Marijn de Vries tweeted a photograph of the podium, and then Lotto tried to shift the blame to local organisers, but the bikini-clad women had been parading through the VIP area during the race, so it's hard to believe that Lotto had no idea what was going on.

The juxtaposition of podium girls with athletes at women's cycling events isn't confined to road racing. BMX Supercross World Cup events – which have the same governing body – adopt the same approach. This is a sport that's grown considerably for all participants since its inclusion in the Beijing Olympics. At the 2016 World Cup event in Argentina, won by Australian Caroline Buchanan, promotional models dressed in head-to-toe lycra stood in front of the winner's podium. Buchanan is not only a five-time BMX and mountain bike world champion, but she's also a campaigner for equal rights in women's sport; her all-girls BMX team, Buchanan Next Gen, provides financial assistance and mentoring to young women in BMX. She was also a strong voice in the push for equal pay at BMX World Cup series events, something that finally came into effect in 2016.

Putting the best possible spin on it, I find it odd and jarring to see elite sportswomen share the same stage as podium girls – I can't help but feel that it takes away from their achievement. It's as though cycling can't celebrate women unless there's a show of traditional femininity nearby.

Ultimately, it's up to the sport's governing body, the International Cycling Union, to act. Women cyclists have worked hard to get to where they are – they deserve better than this. Diminishing the podium of an important women's race to off-cuts from a *Carry On* film does nobody any favours: not the sponsors, not the fans, and certainly not the athletes involved. Hopefully the weight of public opinion, and the opinions of the riders themselves, will finally force a change – the old traditions, much like the breakaway cyclist who's gone too early, are being slowly but surely reeled in and readdressed by the pack. Criticism of the inclusion of podium girls is coming from all angles.

*

'One huuuuundred'n'aaaaaaaaatey ...'

Thanks to increased television coverage, darts is enjoying a surge in popularity – and promotional models dressed in tight-fitting dresses with plunging necklines are very much a part of the pre-match routine. The job of these walk-on girls is to accompany the dart players on their treacherous journey through the crowd, up onto the stage and over to the oche.

Or, as the Bettingpro website puts it in a 2014 post:

> The Premier League Darts is back on our TV screens, which means another chance to check out some of the most beautiful women in sport – the walk-on girls!
>
> The return of the Premier League Darts means the chance to sit in front of the TV on a Thursday night, have a few bets and be thoroughly entertained by one of the most exciting sports around. However, it also has a side benefit, the walk-on girls! Here are our favourites …

Coming in at number seven are Brooke and Lauren Chadwick, one sister in a nurse's uniform, the other in a kitchen apron (with the words 'deviant housewife' on it). Underneath the photo, the caption reads: 'The Chadwick twins are darts [sic] first ever twin walk on girls. And they're twins. Twins!' If there had been a top ten, I'm not sure that the writer of this piece would have made it through without having to excuse himself.

Having walked through the room while my partner has been watching darts (he's a fan of 'the big easy', Raymond Van Barneveld), it's pretty clear that the crowd – dressed as Harry Potter, Nuns, Where's Wally, Dart Boards, Beer Bottles, Storm Troopers, Ninja Turtles, Ronald McDonald, Fred Flintstone, Super Mario, Kiss, Chickens, Jesus, Teletubbies (I'll stop here, but you get the drift) – is having a riotous time. Among all the singing and chanting and bonhomie on view, would they really miss the walk-on girls if they weren't there? I doubt it: darts fans go in a group and they go to have fun, and the atmosphere and colour of the crowd (made up of men and women) just about ensures that – and this is before any actual play or players, or walk-on girls, hit the stage.

Grid girls, podium girls and walk-on girls are not, as some have tried to suggest, anything like the catwalk models of the Melbourne Fashion Festival. Fashion models aren't there simply to add a touch of femininity or to serve the men in the spotlight – they're employed to wear the latest designs. Unlike sport, fashion is an industry where women are well represented in a variety of roles, and the models have an important purpose beyond being ogled by the audience. Most of those who attend Fashion Week are there to celebrate Australian designs, and the models are part of the celebration, not mere garnish.

I see two options: either get men to accessorise women's sport, or do away with the practice altogether. (In a one-off, grid girls were replaced by male models for the 2015 F1 Monaco Grand Prix, much to champion racing driver Sebastian Vettel's disgust.) These sports must move with the times – it's an easy thing to fix if the will is there. Perhaps they could use ambassadors from more than one gender and a whole range of backgrounds … who knows, after the initial grumbling dies down, diverse ambassadors may even attract more bums on seats.

*

Cheerleaders in the National Rugby League are yet another anachronism – one not to be confused with competitive cheerleading. Despite starting out as another form of garnish, cheerleading has developed into a competitive sport, with grades and competitions Australia-wide; competitive cheerleaders perform physically demanding routines that show off their athleticism, agility and skill. But these performances are a far cry from those at men's rugby league matches, where the cheerleaders and their dancing are pure garnish – often with an added sprinkling of titillation.

The culture of the sport is changing slowly, but it is changing. Not long after sexual assault allegations were levelled against members of the Canterbury Bulldogs in 2004, a female member stood up at a Bulldogs AGM and asked when the club was going to give voting rights to women. 'When they play first grade,' then-Bulldogs president Barry 'Punchy' Nelson replied. The events of 2004, as horrendous as they were, set the NRL on a more enlightened path; in that year, Harvey Norman CEO Katie Page became the first woman appointed to the NRL's board. In 2016, the NRL has one female commissioner (Catherine Harris) and the NSW Rugby League has one female board member (Deborah Healey). Across the sixteen NRL clubs, there are thirteen female board members, including two chairwomen (Rebecca Frizelle, Gold Coast Titans; Marina Go, Wests Tigers). Women are a long way from spilling out of the boardroom door, but to the sport's credit, it has taken steps to make its environment more comfortable and welcoming for them.

The NRL's cheerleaders run counter to this: they serve purely as entertainment for men. I've sat in the crowd and seen the reaction that these women get from some men – the whistles, the leering and demeaning comments, all within earshot of young kids. When men act like this, it makes other people feel uncomfortable. Sport should be a fun and inclusive environment, not an unnerving and hostile one.

Some clubs are more progressive than others on this issue. In 2014, Canterbury Bulldogs CEO Raelene Castle reinvented the role of the cheerleader at her club – she turned the resident 'Belles' into 'Sapphires', who now focus on off-field work such as hospital visits and corporate entertainment. In making this decision, Castle said, 'We want to go in a more professional direction, where they do more than just dance in revealing outfits. We want them to be ambassadors and have a much greater role in promoting what this club stands for.' The South Sydney Rabbitohs have led the way here: in 2007, they replaced their cheerleaders with male and female drummers. But most of the clubs are sadly stuck in the past.

It'd be easy to just throw your arms in the air and turn a blind eye to this primitive thinking – there are, after all, much bigger issues on the spectrum of inequality in sport – but it's important to remind ourselves that these things are all connected. Using women as garnishes contributes to the lopsided sporting landscape and further entrenches the attitudes that keep women sidelined in sport.

Anyway, my default position is always optimism. As easy as it is for sport and other institutions to dig their heels in and just keep on doing the same thing – because, well, because that's how it's always been done! – it's heartening to see that traditions once regarded as untouchable are themselves going through a period of introspection.

Outside of sport, even Barbie Dolls are moving with the times: Mattel Inc. is now manufacturing dolls with more realistic bodies. It's a small move, but one that shows that if Barbie – the long-reigning champion of lazy gender stereotypes – can change, then there's hope everywhere.

# 7

## THE WAGE GAP

The gender wage gap in sport exists for the same reason as the gender wage gap in the wider world. Interrelated work, family and societal factors – including stereotypes about the work that women and men 'should' do, and the undervaluing of women's work – keep the pay gap in Australia hovering between 15 and 19 per cent.

Women are paid less than men for doing the same job; women are paid less for doing jobs of equal value; women are paid less because of segregation in the labour market – often linked to traditions and stereotypes. Women are expected to reduce their working hours or leave the labour market to carry out child or elderly care and, on top of all that, domestic responsibilities are still not equally shared, and the task of looking after dependent family members is largely borne by women. Former Prime Minister John Howard wasn't wrong when he told the National Press Club in September 2016 that women would never achieve 50 per cent representation in our parliaments because of their caring roles: he was wrong not to challenge this. The stereotype of woman as carer – the family member who puts everyone else ahead of herself, who happily takes the burnt chicken wing – is a dangerous one. It's what keeps women undervalued and underpaid.

All sectors, sport included, should fight for the principle of equal pay for equal work. It's what underpins a fair society. It not only sustains us financially, but it's also linked to the bigger question of our worth as human beings. And for women in sport, the pay gap is even more staggering than 15 to 19 per cent – it's huge, the kind of gap that rivals the Grand Canyon.

The money in men's professional sport is, to be blunt, obscene. It's been that way for decades, and the commercialisation of sport is making it even bigger. It's obscene that Cristiano Ronaldo will be paid $500,000 in wages by Real Madrid this week; Lionel Messi $476,000 by FC Barcelona; Wayne Rooney $433,000 by Manchester United. It's obscene that LeBron James made $101.4 million in 2016 and Roger Federer made $89.1 million. A little further down, the only Australian in the *Forbes* top hundred richest athletes is golfer Jason Day, in equal sixty-ninth position with $31.58 million. The average AFL salary is $302,104. In 2016, each of the twenty consistent Test players in Australia's national team was given a twelve-month central contract where they're paid a guaranteed yearly retainer fee of $900,000 – and players are also paid match fees for appearing in any Test ($14,000), One-Day International ($7000) or T20 International match ($5000).

At Cricket Australia, the male payment pool is calculated as a percentage of overall revenue – it ranges between 24.5 and 27 per cent depending on performance – and has skyrocketed since the last five-year collective bargaining agreement in 2012. This arrangement was negotiated by the Australian Cricketers' Association (ACA) as part of the players' Memorandum of Understanding (MOU), and it currently weighs in at $70 million. Not a cent of that goes to Australia's women cricketers, who don't have an MOU of their own. Cricket Australia wants to change this so that all players (men and women) are paid out of the same $70 million salary cap. However, the ACA says that the current arrangement for male players should be protected by their MOU. The ACA also argues that if more players are being paid from the same pool, the percentage of revenue that flows towards it should go up so that the men don't lose out. I see their point – the top-ranked male players earn over $2 million a season, and they wouldn't want to see that dented. In response, Cricket Australia has argued that nowhere in the current MOU is there a differentiation between male and female players – the wording is merely 'player' – therefore, Australia's top-performing women can be given a slice of the revenue pie.

Sadly, it's all come down to a game of semantics. No changes have happened yet and, once again, women are still the losers. For the sake of women's cricket, let's hope that all the players are included in the next Australian cricket MOU.

*

Some commentators say that 'the market never lies' (as though the market is a godlike entity incapable of telling an untruth), and that it alone should determine how much sportswomen are paid, but they're looking at this in a very superficial way.

The market doesn't account for attitudes that stop women's sport from flourishing – and those attitudes kick in long before market forces come into play. Using the market as an excuse not to give fair wages simply contributes to the vicious cycle of women's sport being undervalued, which in turn leads to less media coverage, less visibility, lower participation rates, women's sport being undervalued … and around and around we go on some perverse merry-go-round.

The thing about the 'popularity equals more pay' argument is that it only ever seems to apply when men are the ones earning the most money and attention.

The US Women's National Soccer Team's (USWNT's) World Cup victory against Japan in 2015 was the most-watched soccer match in American history. Its viewing figures were also higher than those for every game from the NBA Finals that year. In 2015, the US women's team produced $20 million more in revenue than their men's team – and yet the women players are paid a fraction of what their male counterparts in the men's team earn. This makes a mockery of that argument, which sportswomen have to put up with all the time, that links player wages to revenue. The USWNT is doing better than the men's team on all these measures, yet is paid four times less.

In March 2016, five of the team's most prominent players – Carli Lloyd, Alex Morgan, Hope Solo, Megan Rapinoe and Becky Sauerbrunn – filed a wage-discrimination action with the Equal Employment Opportunity Commission against the US Soccer Federation.

Appearing on NBC's *Today*, Solo said that 'not much has changed' during her time on the team:

I've been on this team for a decade and a half, and I've been through numerous CBA negotiations, and honestly, not much has changed ... We continue to be told we should be grateful just to have the opportunity to play professional soccer, to get paid for doing it ... In this day and age, it's about equality. It's about equal rights. It's about equal pay. We're pushing for that. We believe now the time is right because we believe it's our responsibility for women's sports and specifically for women's soccer to do whatever it takes to push for equal pay and equal rights. And to be treated with respect.

Representing more than just themselves, the American players took aim at the assumption that women athletes should be grateful for having the opportunity to play the sport they love – and the ripples were felt across the globe. Lloyd told the *New York Times:*

Our beef is not with the men's national team; we love those guys, and we support those guys. It's with the Federation, and its history of treating us as if we should be happy that we are professional players and not working in the kitchen or scrubbing the locker room.

This isn't the first time that members of this team have taken a stand against gender inequality – in October 2014, a group including American Abby Wambach, Brazil's Marta and Germany's Nadine Angerer filed a gender discrimination lawsuit against the Canadian Soccer Federation and FIFA, citing the fact that the 2015 World Cup in Canada would be played on artificial turf and not natural grass. They argued that turf is less forgiving; the constant threat of injury affects the way that they play, and balls travel and bounce differently. But, above everything else, this was a matter of equity: the men's World Cup is held on real grass.

In January 2015, the women withdrew their complaint; in a statement, Wambach said it wasn't a waste of time: 'I am hopeful that the players' willingness to contest the unequal playing fields – and the tremendous public support we received during the effort – marks the start of even greater activism to ensure fair treatment when it comes to women's sports.'

*

Getting paid less can also affect the health of women athletes. Between 2007 and 2014, Australian basketball champion Lauren Jackson divided her time between Seattle, Canberra, Russia, Spain, South Korea and China, where she tore her ACL in 2013. She told ABC's 7.30: 'That's the problem with women's sport and why we all get injured and hurt because we have to play 12 months a year so we can make money to live. Whereas men, they play one season and they're good. They can have a break; they can rehab their bodies.'

And what about when a sportswoman falls pregnant? In the cycle of an elite athlete's life, motherhood is the state least compatible with sport. (It's no surprise the parents' club in international tennis is mostly made up of men.) For most sports, motherhood sits in the too-hard basket, and as a consequence athletes either delay having kids or never return to elite sport after giving birth.

That's not to say it's impossible – there's no better example than Evonne Goolagong Cawley, whose second Wimbledon title in 1980 was the first won by a mother since 1914, and more recently we've had netballer Sharelle McMahon, who was well-supported by her sport when she decided to resume playing in 2013 after the birth of her son. Another Australian star, cricketer Sarah Elliott, breastfed her baby Sam at the lunch and tea breaks during an Ashes Test, in which she made her debut century, despite being up most of the night. But these are the exceptions: many others simply can't make it work.

It's hard enough for mothers in 'normal' everyday workplaces: parental leave, childcare (availability and cost), and the work–motherhood juggle are challenges that never seem to go away. Being an elite woman athlete comes with its own set of challenges – the job is physical, the hours are irregular, there are travel demands, and team success is placed above the needs of the individual. On top of all this, the perception that an athlete coming back from having a child will have too many competing demands makes it very difficult for sportswomen to be both mothers and elite athletes.

When Melissa Barbieri announced her pregnancy in 2012, her career as Australia's best goalkeeper crumbled. Without a maternity system in place, she was dropped from the national team and lost all her contracts:

> There is a lot of discrimination against mothers, and that is not just sporting, that is all over the world, that is in every job and it's in every facet of every life. All of a sudden you have a baby and it's like you can't do this or you can't do that. I just want to show mothers out there

that if you want something bad enough, no matter what happens in life you can achieve it just as long as you know what you want.

Barbieri was thrown a lifeline when her friend was named coach of the 'Lady Reds' in Adelaide. He offered her a contract; she travelled between her home town of Melbourne and Adelaide for two seasons; she got noticed by national selectors and was named in the 2015 FIFA World Cup squad as number two goalkeeper to Lydia Williams:

> Coming back from having a baby makes you a stronger person, and it doesn't need to be feared ... it doesn't disrupt a team but it brings the team closer together, and once coaches see the positive impact children can have on a team then I'm sure they won't mind having more around the team environment.

*

It boils down to common sense and decency – both of which were sorely lacking in the decision to fly the Australian women's basketball team economy to the London Olympics while the men flew business.

This kind of thinking isn't reserved for basketball. Further investigation at the time revealed that the Matildas and Southern Stars also flew economy while their male counterparts enjoyed the benefits of being seated away from the tail and on the good side of the curtain: 'Yes, I will have another cheese platter, thank you.'

Nobody could argue that success had anything to do with the decision to keep the women's basketball team in economy – the Opals have won three silver medals and two bronze at five of the past six Olympics, while the Boomers have come agonisingly close but have never won an Olympic medal. The Opals reportedly tried to lobby for better treatment and continually asked Basketball Australia to justify its decision, only to hear that it was because the men's team had got better funding. But they didn't stop there: they also justified their decision by saying that the men needed more space because they were bigger. We're talking about the women's basketball team here – Liz Cambage is 203 centimetres tall.

Getting worked up about seating arrangements on a long-haul flight may seem trivial, and Liz Cambage and Lauren Jackson could afford to upgrade, but that's not really the point. If the people in charge can't see that simple stuff like this creates a two-tier system where the women are clearly less valued, then it makes you wonder about their ability to sort out the more important stuff.

We know that the bigger sports are locked into a way of thinking that's been entrenched; a mindset that feasts on the assumption that sport is men's business. Women are automatically treated second to men because, well, that's the way it's always been – with the tacked-on notion that what you make from the game or your sport should only ever reflect what you bring to it financially (well, at least when men are making the most money). What's missing here is a serious conversation about what sort of society we want, and how these inequalities could possibly align with that vision.

I want a society where women are paid equally to men,

and a society where sport isn't just the domain of men. Paying sportswomen fairly will get us closer to both. Healthy, vibrant women's competitions where the athletes are paid and valued enough to dedicate themselves to their sport, matched with support from media and commercial partners, will make pursuing a career in sport more attractive to girls.

The cycle we want is more attention leading to more grassroots players leading to a bigger audience, and on and on it goes – a much healthier merry-go-round!

There will always be people who argue that women's sport doesn't deserve more money because the men's game earns the money; some go further and say that this is true equality. As more and more women pull on footy jumpers and cricket pads, these uninformed attitudes will become irrelevant, but until we make it to that point, we have to give women's sport the support it needs to smash through all remaining barriers. When it does, a whole new world of opportunities will open up for women who play and love sport – a world without the taint of misogyny.

# 8

## THE DARK UNDERBELLY

The time I came closest to taking a sabbatical from sport was in 2004, when incidents associated with two footy codes took the shine off all sports for me. I know that this is completely irrational, like breaking up with someone and then turning against everyone of that sex, but sport is an emotional business and, rightly or wrongly, I just didn't feel the same about it then.

My growing unease wasn't with the game itself. My love of Australian Rules has never faded, and that's despite the Crows' gut-wrenching five-point loss to Hawthorn in the 2012 preliminary finals coming after their consecutive preliminary final losses to West Coast in 2005 and 2006. What a game! My head almost exploded watching Graham Johncock's goal on the run to put the Crows ahead in the last quarter, and then it almost exploded again (a different kind of eruption – the grief of a sports tragic) as Ben Stratton put a match-winning tackle on Patrick Dangerfield. When I slumped in my seat, tears welling, my partner squeezed my hand gently, then leaned over and whispered, 'Keep your dignity.'

As painful as these kinds of losses are, they don't erode my faith in the game. Nor do I share the view that football has become wrapped in cotton wool and is the worse for it.

Typical pub conversation, mid-evening: 'All you have to do is stare at someone these days and you give away a fifty. The game's gone soft.'

'D'you remember when Thommo got both his legs broken in the first quarter? It didn't stop him kicking ten straight and taking mark of the year. Remember the way he swung his spine around his head as he was carried off the field on Johnno's shoulders?'

'Pure courage, there wasn't a dry eye in the house.'

As society evolves, so do our attitudes to on-field violence, and the game's rules must evolve to reflect that: just as footy culture is evolving to combat violence off the field.

At the far end of the sexism spectrum – on the flip side of casual sexism – is the ultimate, darkest manifestation of hyper-masculine sporting culture. It shows just how poorly women can be treated in this male-dominated environment; it's the very worst symptom of gender asbestos, and it has caused women to turn off sport.

For girlfriends of mine who've somehow lived full lives while only having a passing interest in football, the events of that year were the last straw. After years of faking an interest in footy just to fit in with the rest of us, they dropped it altogether without too much internal wrangling. Those of us with more than a passing interest in either the AFL or NRL went through something more introspective and painful.

In 2004, the dark side of two very masculine sports was laid bare for all to see: women were, for some of these sportsmen, pieces of meat. We learnt how widespread and acceptable the practice of using and sharing women for sex was. Those who hadn't believed, or had chosen not to believe, that there was a predatory side to footy culture had to confront an ugly truth.

The allegations also led to widespread conjecture as to why these two sports seemed to attract this kind of behaviour. My suspicion is that it's no coincidence. Rugby league and Australian Rules often have common elements: a super-macho 'no chicks allowed' attitude mixed with a team mentality that encourages 'bonding' in the most private and intimate environments, and a whole lot of hero-worshipping (by all fans) that encourages players to feel untouchable and entitled to their 'fun'. When these factors coexist – and specific action isn't taken to combat this dangerous cocktail – you are left with a large group of young men living without the sort of reality checks and consequences that exist in other spaces.

*

The incidents of 2004 are too revolting and distasteful, not to mention legally fraught, to go into in detail. They involved multiple players at multiple clubs in multiple male-only codes, and allegations by numerous women of sexual abuse, rape and gang rape. The stories also have in common a culture of cover-up by many of the clubs themselves, hamstrung police procedures, a Jekyll and Hyde media, and an overall sense of how incredibly difficult it is for these women to get any sort of justice. I was left feeling sickened by it all.

As I sat down to watch Ticky Fullerton's *Four Corners* report in 2004, it hit me: the heaviness, the sadness and the anger. Women telling their stories, club people squirming out of responsibility, rugby league players talking about the culture of the 'bun' or 'gangbanging', women treated like meat, hush money, victim blaming, how cases like these never get to a jury. It all painted a horrific picture that made me feel ashamed to be associated with footy. Friends – not only women – quizzed me about my passion: 'How can you continue to support this? You realise that by going along every week, you're complicit.'

I found it hard to walk through the turnstiles. But as a sports reporter in Melbourne, this was my job from February to September. Melbourne moves to the beat of the AFL drum: every result, injury, indiscretion and fart gets covered. It was my job to report on every aspect of the game – and during 2004, a lot of my time was spent talking and writing about rape and sexual assault allegations.

As a fan, I had a choice. I could've walked, but I didn't. I felt conflicted and I was bloody furious, but ... I couldn't turn my back on the game that I loved. My pappou discovered Australian Rules shortly after he arrived off the boat from Greece in the 1940s; he passed on his love of it to my mum, and she passed on her love to my brother and me. This game is a living breathing part of my life, and it's been like that for as long as I can remember. I couldn't let football go. I just hoped that things would change.

In response to the spate of allegations, AFL CEO Andrew Demetriou called on all women with a story to tell to come forward. Not everyone applauded the AFL's stance. Former

Carlton president John Elliott thought that it would create more headaches than it was worth. He told *Four Corners*:

> You know, it may re-raise things that have been long forgotten. Therefore it's not going to help the football club, it won't help some of the … the players that may have been involved. And I just can't imagine why he did it. But I think it was, you know, maybe just the media scrutiny – that he wants to be holier than thou.

Holier than thou? For encouraging women to pursue justice for sexual assault or rape?

In 2009, at a charity fundraiser in Hobart, Elliott reportedly told the audience that women who alleged they were raped by Carlton players in the 1980s and '90s were paid hush money. It wasn't the first time I'd heard claims of this nature; sadly, I've heard a few stories about hush money, intimidation and police influence in football. It's impossible to say whether all or any of these factors are behind each case, but that's beside the point – somehow, footballers keep getting accused of rape and sexual assault, and while some charges have been laid, none have led to successful prosecutions. Police interviewed Elliott about his claims that the club covered up allegations of sexual assault: nothing came of it.

Not all football culture is toxic, of course. To paint it as such would be grossly untrue and unfair. So much of what happens inside a footy club, whether NRL or AFL or at the grassroots level, is positive. Footy can teach physical discipline, the benefits of teamwork, hard work, fair play, resilience, leadership, the importance of community work. It can open the eyes of players to the less fortunate through club-sponsored charity work, and show them the importance of being role models and upstanding members of the community. Lifelong friendships are formed as teams are given the opportunity to play a game they love in front of adoring fans. Players can experience the purity of great sport played at the highest level.

But you'd need to have your head stuck so far down in the sand that you're sniffing magma not to acknowledge that there's a problematic element to hyper-masculine team sports. A dark, perverse kind of bonding is based on humiliating, sexually objectifying and degrading women. Treating women as objects, whether verbally or physically, is used as a deranged way to forge closeness, acting to validate not only a shared team identity, but also to provide proof of being 'real men': the type of men who win. Passing around a woman in a group-sex session that ranges from the questionably consensual to unmistakeable gang rape is the sickening pinnacle of a dysfunctional and warped culture. Rugby league players have even admitted that group sex is a bonding activity; the women involved barely get a mention – they're reduced to the role of 'bun'.

In this dark side of footy culture, there's limited understanding of the idea that no means no, or that something that starts off as consensual and turns into something else is abhorrent.

*

The stench around the two football codes lingered for years, and new incidents added to the unsavoury brew – some were less serious, but still revolting.

In 2009, seven North Melbourne players produced a video

124

called 'The Adventures of Little Boris', which features a condom-clad rubber chicken performing sex acts to a gangster rap song titled 'Move Bitch'. It includes scenes with a 'female' chicken being thrown against a wall and run over by a vehicle, before the 'male' has sex with its carcass. This video was only meant for in-house eyes, but it found its way to YouTube. The North Melbourne club fined two senior players over their part in the video; the club also disciplined the staff member responsible for its publication on the internet. The players involved apologised and appeared genuinely remorseful.

I was on breakfast radio at the time, and this incident was quite a talking point. Remarkably, some people couldn't see the link between the video and the part of footy culture that degrades and demeans women. The symbolism of a female chook being thrown against a wall, run over by a car and sexually abused wasn't stark enough for some. I was told to 'lighten up'. Here's how the *Herald Sun*'s Superfooty reported it, in what was intended to be a humorous piece: 'BORIS the rubber chicken has broken his silence on the chook-sex video scandal that this week rocked AFL club North Melbourne.'

I suppose if we lived in a society where women were just as valued and respected as men and weren't used as playthings by some footballers, the *Sun* may have had a point: the video could have just been a silly joke made by silly boys to entertain themselves, with no connection to actual sexual assault. But nothing is ever truly out of context, and if these footballers had any real understanding of (or at least cared about) how badly women have been treated by men within their sport, they would have seen how unsettling and problematic this video is. That it didn't occur to them that a footballer making fun of rape is a big no-no may be a sign of stupidity and insensitivity, sure, but more worrying is that clearly they just weren't getting the message. And saying, 'It's fine, they didn't mean it like that, mountain out of a molehill,' as was the response of many of our talkback callers, doesn't do anything to help get that message across either.

Jokes about rape and domestic violence are never funny. This view is not only shared by the so-called 'PC brigade' and Mark Latham's 'left feminist clique' – just ask the police officers who attend, on average, six hundred cases of family violence a day across the country, with a call-out once every two minutes to help a woman being controlled, abused and harmed. Just ask the doctors at our major hospitals, and the women who comfort and care for domestic violence survivors in crisis accommodation. Sexist slogans like the ones used by company Wicked Campers ('in every princess there's a little slut who wants to try it just once'), sexist T-shirts and 'jokes' are not harmless because, when combined with pre-existing sexist attitudes, they can normalise threatening and hostile behaviour towards women. Not only is this dangerous, it also stops any kind of positive change.

*

The events of 2004 led to a perfect storm of media coverage, which drew attention not only to the players involved, but also to their football codes. And they led to community backlash.

The AFL quickly responded to the negative publicity by embarking on a campaign to position itself as socially responsible and prepared to stand up against all forms of violence against women. This was enshrined in a new policy known as 'Respect and Responsibility'. Launched in November 2005, the policy's broad intention is to 'firmly position the AFL as a leader in advocating cultural change that will lead to safe and inclusive environments for women and girls, across all levels of Australian Football'. Components of the policy included: the introduction of model anti-sexual-harassment and anti-sexual-discrimination procedures across the AFL and its sixteen clubs; training and education for AFL players; changes to the player rules governing 'conduct unbecoming'; the development of resources for community clubs to ensure safe, supportive environments for women and girls; and the development of an AFL-led public education campaign. The AFL player training involves the delivery of a ninety-minute, one-off session on respectful relationships and bystander behaviours.

The NRL had a different response: they engaged researchers to determine whether any aspects of rugby league culture encouraged or condoned violence against women. The findings of this research led to a collaboration between the NRL, the research team and Moira Carmody from the University of Western Sydney, who had developed a program for young people called 'Sex and Ethics'.

In 2009, the Sex and Ethics program was piloted with NRL players and subsequently rolled out. The six-session education program addresses attitudes, skills to negotiate sexual intimacy, the impact of alcohol and drugs on decision-making, ethical consent and the law, and bystander behaviour.

Since the introduction of these programs, there have been far fewer cases of sexual assault associated with both types of football.

In 2010, one of the incidents from 2004 began to make headlines once again. The news came from two former detectives at Brighton police station who had investigated sexual assault allegations against St Kilda footballers Steven Milne and Leigh Montagna back in 2004. They claimed that there had been attempts from within the station to sabotage the investigation – that recordings of interviews with Milne and Montagna had been taken from one of the officer's desks and that the alleged victim's statement had been leaked to St Kilda Football Club. After a raid of the Brighton criminal investigation unit, Victoria Police's ethical standards department confirmed that there was a significant amount of evidence missing from the case against Milne.

In 2012, the Office of Police Integrity (OPI) called for a review of the 2004 evidence by the specialist sex crime squad. While the OPI later released a report that held there was no specific evidence of interference or inappropriate influence, Assistant Commissioner Stephen Fontana was still 'extremely disappointed' at how the investigation had been handled by Victoria Police, a sentiment that was eventually backed up by Victoria Police itself, in a 2013 statement conceding that the original investigation had been 'substantially inadequate'.

Eventually, after twelve months of gathering evidence, and with Milne having retired from professional football, the sex crime squad decided to charge him with four counts of rape.

At the committal hearing in the Melbourne Magistrates Court, the court heard that the complainant had thought she was having sex in a darkened bedroom with Milne's then-teammate Montagna, with whom she'd had consensual sex earlier that night. Prosecutor David Cordy told the court that

Milne continued having sex with the then nineteen-year-old after she, still believing he was Montagna, repeatedly said 'no' and attempted to make him wear a condom. Cordy said that it was only after a naked Montagna and the complainant's friend entered the room, having had consensual sex in another room, that the woman realised she was with Milne. He said that she then retreated to a bathroom with her friend, saying she felt sick and repeating, 'I thought it was Leigh.'

Cordy told the court that Montagna had sent a text message to the complainant the following day, saying, 'Sorry about what happened last night. I thought you knew it was him and not me.' Montagna said he'd heard the woman say 'no', but there was no change in the 'friendly' atmosphere in the room. 'He [Milne] just said, "sweet, no problem", or something like that,' Montagna told the court. But the other woman present in the room said that she felt intimidated and opened the door when she heard her friend say 'no' to Milne.

Milne was to face trial for three rape charges in 2014, but the charges were discontinued. Instead, Milne pleaded guilty to a single charge of indecent assault. He avoided conviction and was fined $15,000.

You would think that these events would have put an end to any support from sporting culture for any man accused of assaulting a woman. But they didn't. In November 2015, the Red Cliffs Tigers appointed former AFL footballer Nick Stevens as their senior football coach, despite him having been found guilty in January 2015 of assaulting his girlfriend; Stevens was found guilty of twelve charges, including making threats to kill and assault his former partner. In March 2015, he was sentenced to eight months in jail but walked free on bail after his lawyers lodged an appeal against his conviction and sentence. In a statement at the time of his appointment, the Red Cliff Tigers said that they were 'extremely excited to have Nick on board and are looking forward to him bringing his skills and knowledge to the club for both senior and junior club development'.

Fortunately, AFL Victoria intervened to stop him coaching the Tigers, and the Sunraysia Football and Netball League refused to grant him registration as a coach or player until the criminal matters were dealt with. He abandoned his appeal and agreed to plead guilty to two charges of intentionally causing serious injury as part of a plea deal that saw the other ten charges dropped. In July 2016, he was jailed for three months and fined $3000.

*

In order to change attitudes and wipe toxic elements from football culture, strong leadership must be shown when dealing with all cases, on and off the field, that demean and disrespect women.

In 2011, West Coast's Patrick McGinnity sledged Melbourne forward Ricky Petterd, saying he was going to rape Petterd's mother – a disgusting comment that he repeated twice as the teams left the field for half-time. His punishment was a week's suspension, a $2500 fine, and counselling on the AFL's Respect and Responsibility policies. McGinnity's manager, ex-footballer David Sierakowski, claimed that this punishment was over the top and said that Petterd should be ashamed for alerting the umpire: 'To have a Melbourne player come out and do this to him is quite embarrassing. If Ricky Petterd had his time over again, I think he'd do it differently.' Sierakowski also accused Petterd of being 'thin-skinned'. If Sierakowski, a player manager responsible for shaping the lives of the men under his guidance, cannot understand how the words 'I'll rape your mum' have no place in the game, then herein lies the problem.

It's not the sports themselves that lead to a culture of disrespect towards women, but sexist attitudes that breed among peers in male team sports. A considerable amount of research has been done in the USA and Canada on this topic – some of the factors that have been hypothesised to increase male players' risks of perpetrating sexual assault are: male bonding, aggressive sport, the sexualisation and subordination of women (as garnish or as supporters and carers), celebrity status and entitlement, excessive alcohol use and other drug abuse and 'groupie' culture. The AFL refers to this research in its Respect and Responsibility program: 'Building Cultures of Respect and Non-Violence.'

The challenge for our football codes is to break down attitudes that can lead to violence against women. Players need to be educated about the definition of rape. They need to call out antiquated behaviours and attitudes, and they also need exposure to women in and around their football club – women in a whole range of roles, who can offer another kind of leadership, as well as advice.

St Kilda has taken big steps to achieve this by proactively promoting gender equality. Under CEO Matt Finnis, the club has transformed its once hyper-masculine culture into one that celebrates diversity in all its forms. This forward-thinking ideology has led to the appointment of several women executives, general managers, board members and the first woman – Peta

Searle – to an AFL club coaching panel in 2014. In 2016, every female member of St Kilda's staff took part in a three-month empowerment program to encourage them to speak up and aspire to the top jobs. Everything that St Kilda is doing to make the club more inclusive points to real cultural change.

A lot of good has come from the pain of 2004. Both codes have been forced into doing something about the dark side of footy culture, and the allegations were a light-bulb moment for some fans – but unfortunately not for all. Some still see the game as purely macho, and sexist sledging, cheap 'jokes' and cases of assault against women all trumpet the idea that sport is a space for men only.

It's understandable that many women don't even want to try to enter this space. I've felt that way myself sometimes – alienated from the sport that I love, disappointed and disillusioned. And I haven't always been as outspoken about these issues as I am now.

# 9

## COMPLICITY

When a man gives his opinion, he's a man. When a
woman gives her opinion, she's a bitch.

*Bette Davis*

Of all the sports functions I've attended over the years (and
there have been many), one sticks out in my memory for all
the wrong reasons. Towards the end of the evening, I went to
the ladies' room. When I came out of my cubicle and headed
for the washbasin, I saw a man leaning against the wall. And
he was staring at me. I knew him (he's well known in sporting
circles), and I'd been speaking to him earlier in the night. The
sight of him stopped me dead in my tracks. He registered the
look of confusion on my face and offered up a smile. He then
unzipped himself and pulled out his penis.

It's not like me to be lost for words, but moments like this
freeze the brain. Mine iced up in about half a blink, leaving me
at the mercy of my autopilot – which fortunately walked me

right out of the bathroom door just as the rush of blood to my head almost blinded me. My last memory of the encounter is of him standing there with his appendage framed against his grey suit trousers, his glazed eyes, and his smile rapidly fading from his face.

I started breathing again once I found sanctuary in the quiet shadows outside the function room. *What the hell just happened? Did he really do that?* I laughed as a reflex, but I was shaken. I held my hand out in front of me – an instinctual test – my fingers trembling, adrenaline zinging through my blood. I slipped away from the function, then spent the rest of the night and some time afterwards trying to get my head around what had occurred. I'd just been flashed. Not by a stranger in the saltbushes near the beach: but by someone I knew.

I didn't confront him at the time. And I didn't tell anyone at the function what had happened. What did he think he was doing? What was going through his head as he made his way towards the women's toilets? 'Hey, I'll show Ange something that'll really break the ice.' What did he want? A round of applause? For me to invite him into the cubicle for further examination? Was it his way of flirting? (99.9 per cent of women would find being flashed about as attractive as watching someone lose control of their bowels during an intimate dinner.) I certainly didn't flirt with him, so there was no way that he could have misinterpreted our earlier conversation – not that this would be excusable. At the end of the day, if someone is going to show me his business, I want to have some say in the matter.

I'm not prudish, so what was so interesting and disturbing

for me was that I felt really rattled by the incident; I never once felt threatened, but I certainly felt violated. I couldn't help wondering how a father would feel about his daughter being exposed (in all senses of the word) to that kind of behaviour. What would a brother do if he heard that it had happened to his sister? How would you feel if it happened to your mother or your best friend?

I talked to friends of mine about it and was shocked to hear how many of them had suffered a similar experience at some point in their lives – at work, a work party or after-work drinks … I was also surprised to learn that they hadn't said anything about it. I'm not suggesting that this flaunting of the organ is common practice – most guys I know would be horrified by it – but what strikes a chord with me is how many others also felt compromised about speaking out, even though they knew it was an outrageously inappropriate thing to do and that some kind of action should be taken.

Let's be real, though. It's never simple to speak out about uncomfortable things – most people take a deep breath, then weigh up the pros and cons (because there are always pros and cons). We all want to get by, and we all want to fit in. We get by on the choices that we make – we do this and we get accepted, we do that and we don't. What's going to happen if I say this? What will the reaction be? It gets complicated, and part of the problem is that we're often forced to shift our moral boundaries to get by, to be liked, to feel part of a group. We're all forced into complicity, though perhaps for different reasons depending on our gender.

I didn't confront the man (I should have) and I didn't tell his peers (I should have), and I'm not going to name him here (maybe I should, but I'd rather play the ball than the man on this occasion).

I knew that it was more trouble than it was worth. I was new on the scene in Melbourne, the sporting capital of Australia: I knew that my story would label me, I knew it would follow me everywhere, I knew it would set me further apart from my peers in sport. I already felt like an outsider – as a woman and, even worse, a woman from *Adelaide*. I was trying to carve out a career in sport in a new city, and the last thing I wanted to do was to further ostracise myself.

So I opted for the way of the three wise monkeys: hear nothing, see nothing and say nothing. Some would call this 'cowardly', some 'smart'. And some would call it 'necessary'. I left my conscience behind and I buried my values deep – something I would do over and over again in work situations to keep relationships intact. I knew that by turning a blind eye to one of the darker elements of sporting culture, I was compromising my values. It was a conscious decision to just get on with those around me, to make my work life as comfortable as possible and kick career goals. I didn't feel great about it.

*

Most women have a story about wanting to speak out against something they thought was wrong, but not going through with it. Most women have witnessed behaviour that's left them feeling compromised. Most women have said what needed to be said inside their heads and kept their mouths shut – because in the real world (not our fantasy world where we're bulletproof) speaking out on matters of sexism and inequality often marks you as a troublemaker: a fire starter, a poor sport (how ironic), not one of the gang, an uptight bitch, a femmo, a prude, a killjoy. Sometimes it's just easier to go along with things.

The sad reality for girls is that this kind of deal with the devil starts early. Girls are encouraged to 'be nice', to please, to be quiet, to accept intrusions and impositions and insults without causing fuss – especially when they're made by men in powerful positions.

Academics, feminists, writers and sociologists have been debating women and complicity for decades. French philosopher Simone de Beauvoir's most famous and influential work, *The Second Sex* (1949), is one of the earliest attempts to confront human history from a feminist perspective. It won her many admirers and just as many detractors. In it, she argues that men oppress women by characterising them, on every level, as the 'Other'. Women aren't *born* feminine but socially constructed that way – conditioned into accepting passivity, dependence, repetition and inwardness.

> The fact is that men encounter more complicity in their woman companions than the oppressor usually finds in the oppressed; and in bad faith they use it as a pretext to declare that woman wanted the destiny they imposed on her. We have seen that in reality her whole education conspires to bar her from paths of revolt and adventure; all of society – beginning with her respected parents – lies to her in extolling the high value of love, devotion, and the gift of self and in concealing the fact that neither lover, husband, nor children will be disposed to bear the burdensome responsibility of it.

She cheerfully accepts these lies because they invite her to take the easy slope ...

Since de Beauvoir's masterwork, society has evolved, though with that evolution has come new types of complicity. Women aren't as shackled to one particular notion of femininity as we were – we're carving out careers for ourselves and forging ahead in male-dominated fields like finance, politics and sport – but clearly it's still hard to change culture.

Former Victorian Police commissioner Ken Lay cried when he read, in a survey of community attitudes towards family violence, that girls as young as ten are diminishing the seriousness of abuse they receive from boys. The 2015 National Community Attitudes towards Violence Against Women Survey, commissioned by the Federal Government, shows that while 96 per cent of Australians condemn domestic violence, underlying attitudes entrench the problem. It found that blaming the victim is so automatic that many people don't realise they're doing it. Lay, now chair of the COAG Advisory Panel on Reducing Violence against Women and Children, said that despite his years leading Victoria's police force, he was shocked and saddened by the survey:

When presented with some scenarios of aggression by boys, I heard with sadness about ten-year-old girls already diminishing the abuse they received from boys. I heard girls say about boys harassing them: 'It's not that bad, it's not like he punched her.' I heard boys justifying the violence by saying that they just wanted to be heard, that it was harmless.

How often do we hear 'boys will be boys'? These children don't know that they're complicit in perpetuating gender stereotypes: it's what they see and what they hear.

Left unchecked, these attitudes are carried into their teenage years. I remember the lengths that some girls went to, trying to be popular with the boys at school. These girls distanced themselves from their bookish or 'nerdy' friends, and some very athletic girls dropped out of sport because they were 'too cool for it'. Every action was done to please the boys – even if it meant compromising themselves and their ability to express themselves.

For women in a male-dominated workplace, it's usually not about impressing the boys with your femininity: it's about 'being one of the boys'. The temptation to 'go with the flow' when you don't agree is a hell of a lot stronger than in other parts of life. You're a rare female voice, so the last thing on earth you want to do is speak out against anything – let alone anything that has a whiff of controversy.

Even speaking out in a gentle way about inequality in sport can be more trouble than it's worth. In 2014, Melbourne radio station Triple M celebrated a ratings win by tweeting a publicity photo of its on-air team – the photo included twenty-five men and no women. I responded to the photo with my own tweet: 'A gorgeous gathering but I can't quite put my finger on what's missing. #oestrogen'. Soon afterwards, I received an SMS from one of the station managers, telling me how my tweet had soured their celebrations – I wonder what he would have messaged me if I'd gone harder!

\*

I've had the complicity conversation with many women in sport over the years, and it never changes much. Deep down, we've all felt complicit at one time or another – whether it's in ignoring inappropriate behaviour of the groping kind, sexist 'jokes' or innuendo. As Hillary Clinton said in 1994:

> There's that kind of double bind that women find themselves in. On the one hand, yes, be smart, stand up for yourself. On the other hand, don't offend anybody, don't step on toes, or you'll become somebody that nobody likes because you're too assertive.

Trailblazing women have to work very hard to be respected. They carry not only their own hopes but also the hopes of other women in their field, and they feel intense pressure not to screw up. If a guy stuffs up, he stuffs up; if a woman stuffs up and she's the *only* woman, then her suitability for the role is far more likely to be called into question.

In 2014, Wallabies utility back Kurtley Beale sent two lewd messages containing pictures of obese women to teammates, accidentally copying in the Wallabies business manager, Di Patston. One message was captioned simply: 'Di', the other, 'Di who wants a go fucking this?' In a series of text messages between Beale and Patston in the hours after the incident, Beale begged Patston for forgiveness. Patston agreed to give him a second chance and not show the texts to coach Ewen McKenzie or the Australian Rugby Union.

These words from Patston particularly resonate with me: 'Do you realise the situation you've put me in? I have earned this job and I am proud of being a female at this level. If I complain then I make it hard for women in rugby.' They encapsulate how many women feel when they reach a position of power and influence in a male-dominated field. The last thing you want to do is fail.

I was the first woman to co-host a sports breakfast radio show in Melbourne, and I saw this as both an honour and a responsibility: no woman had been invited there before me. I have fond memories of my time there and formed a bond with my male co-hosts, who I consider my friends (when you start work at 5am, you form a certain solidarity with your co-workers, the only other people to truly understand the hell your body goes through just to make it in on time every day, let alone get the brain fired up). I also loved the listeners – many weren't too happy with me coming on board, but fortunately I managed to win most of them over.

The whole time I was there, I was very aware of being 'a woman' – and I put up with crap that I wouldn't tolerate now. For instance, wearing a bunny suit isn't my idea of fun, but that's what I found myself in shortly after I joined Radio Sport 927. I'm not sure which bright spark came up with the idea, but the 'request' was put to me on air and enthusiastically taken up by everyone in the studio. And it was backed by management. I repeatedly said that I didn't want to do it, though I knew they wouldn't take no for an answer. I was told that male hosts had done it before me; I found out later that this wasn't true. So I became 'Lenny the Lure' – a life-size version of the bait that greyhounds chase at the races. The rabbit costume was heavy, hot and very awkward to get around in. I had a designated guide to stop me from falling over while I was paraded in front of the punters as a giant, white, uncoordinated, sweating rabbit wobbling through the dining room and the trackside presentation area. I wore it for an hour. Feeling hot and uncomfortable was only part of it – I felt embarrassed and unprofessional. Almost two decades in the media, and there I was being led around a greyhound track dressed as a fucking rabbit for the amusement of (mostly) men.

Dressing up as a giant bunny sits at the lesser end of the complicity scale, but it neatly captures the internal wrangling of a woman working in a man's world. Unless you're a woman or a member of a minority group, it's difficult to understand how compromising such an environment can be.

*

If women in leadership openly complain about gender bias, they run the risk of being vilified by colleagues, competitors and the media for 'playing the gender card'.

In 2012, Prime Minister Julia Gillard made a speech in parliament attacking what she called Opposition Leader Tony Abbott's 'misogyny'. This received global attention and became known as the 'Misogyny Speech'. Commenting on the speech on ABC TV's 7.30, Senator Penny Wong highlighted the backlash that keeps women silent:

This is what happens when women name what's happening. People use ways, and they are either, 'you're being a victim', 'you're trying to cover up your incompetence', 'you're just being politically correct' – these are all tactics to silence women when we speak out about what is really happening. It's not a new tactic. I think most of us who've had to confront sexism in our lives, in our workplaces, are familiar with it.

This sense of not wanting to rock the boat is perhaps greatest in team sport. In the lead-up to the London Olympics, Australian swimmers Eamon Sullivan, Matt Targett, James Magnussen, James Roberts, Tommaso D'Orsogna and Cameron McEvoy took part in a 'bonding' session that involved taking the sleeping drug Stilnox. Despite inconsistencies in accounts, it seems that some time after midnight a group of male swimmers started making prank phone calls to female swimmers' rooms and knocking on their doors.

Olympic swim team member Jade Neilsen spoke out to the media about the relay team's behaviour towards her and another female teammate that night, saying that it was 'completely inappropriate ... so inappropriate it was not funny'. Another member of the swim team, Emily Seebohm, also complained to the Australian team's head coach Leigh Nugent. But no further action was taken.

Shortly after Jade Neilsen spoke publicly, another female swimmer, Cate Campbell, was put on the spot by *The Today Show*. Clearly uncomfortable about answering any questions on the incident, she eventually offered the line: 'Boys will be boys.'

Despite confirming they found the behaviour obnoxious and disruptive, the female swimmers stopped short of calling it harassment and chose not to pursue the matter under Swimming Australia's ethical behaviour by-laws. Although Neilsen was willing to speak out about what had happened in general terms, she refused to be specific about the allegations. Her roommate on the night in question had her name withheld in the media, presumably because of an unwillingness to publicly come forward. No other female swimmers have spoken publicly about what happened.

Whichever way you look at it, there appears to have been a disturbing cone of silence around the incident. Can you imagine the uproar if the girls had hassled the boys in the same way? Dawn Fraser still gets grief for stealing a flag in Tokyo – and that was in 1964.

*

There's another side of complicity that keeps the wheels of sexist sporting culture turning: male complicity. Women can absolutely make a difference by challenging norms, but there's a limit to how much can be achieved when your views aren't equally respected and you don't have the same decision-making clout. Men have the power to smash the paradigm, if the will is there. They have a birthright to an opinion in sport, so they're more likely to be taken seriously and listened to, and this puts them in a privileged position to drive meaningful change. Men have the opportunity – and I'd say responsibility – to think about this stuff and try to counter it.

But many men don't take this opportunity. Some remain quiet because they don't care, and the 'natural' order of things suits them down to the ground; others are pushed to shut up and play along for the sake of the team (this is the kind of behaviour that, at its worst, leads to sexual assault going unchallenged in group situations); and others don't act for the same reason that women don't – it's seen as a backwards or, at the very least, a sideways career move. The bottom line is that when men stay silent, it's women who often bear the consequences of that silence.

Most of us like to think that we're moral people who make consistently moral decisions. So it's no surprise that many men in sport (and some women, too) feel the need to come out swinging whenever the unfair treatment of women is mentioned. Being shown our own complicity can be challenging, and sometimes it's easier to dismiss the whole issue than to accept that we're part of the problem. We need to be able to acknowledge that just because we have ethics, this doesn't mean that we always follow them. Sometimes the moral compass goes AWOL. Other things get in the way. I don't smoke, but I was happy to pretend I did because the man offering me a cigarette (on that that warm and starlit summer evening in Adelaide) was Ayrton Senna. I took the smoke, and he lit it for me. We were alone, and I was trying not to stare at his velvet brown eyes, and I was trying to pretend that I smoked, and I was trying to be cool and not cough as I inhaled. Morals? It's Ayrton Senna! And, holy shit, he's flirting. Take another drag, Ange. Blow a smoke ring, chain-smoke, pull out a bloody cigar ...

But when it comes to inequality in sport, the greatest factor that messes with our morals isn't charismatic Brazilian superstars – it's patriarchy.

Unfortunately, there's no magic wand to wave and no spell to break. The only way forward is for all of us to speak out. And we all know how tough that can be. If I had my time again, I wish I could say that I'd speak up after every sexist or demeaning comment, after every unasked-for grope, kiss and drunken lunge – but honestly, I'd probably keep my mouth shut again. What I can do now, with the benefit of a stronger voice, is make the case for why it's important for women in sport to speak out and how we should do it. The first step is to cast our eyes further. We're not lone voices. As women in sport, we're part of something much bigger: we're connected to a worldwide movement to improve the lives of girls and women, and we should draw strength from that.

# PART TWO

# The Tipping Point

# 10

## GAME CHANGERS

> I will not be lectured about sexism and misogyny by
> this man. I will not. And the Government will not
> be lectured about sexism and misogyny by this man.
> Not now, not ever.
>
> *Julia Gillard*

It feels good to be comfortable in my own skin. It took a while
to get here, but I made it in one piece. I've reached a place where
I can call out sexism and not be fearful of the reprisals. I've
found my voice, and it's strong. I'm me again. The nine-year-
old Angela has made a triumphant return (minus the tracksuit).
Being a freelance journalist helps: I'm not shackled to one
organisation and its views. But I also think my changed attitude
has a lot to do with becoming a mother.

Deep down, I'd always wanted to be a mother. This feeling,
the desire to have a child, wasn't something I spoke about (or
quietly obsessed about, either) – there wasn't some grand master

plan that I mapped out in my head before drifting off to sleep each night. In my head (which was far too busy with working hard and playing hard) I just assumed that it would happen – life would unfold and the rest would take care of itself. Easy.

Only in my late thirties did I start to think that it might never happen, and only then did I realise quite how much it meant to me. I'd buried any feelings about motherhood in red wine, work, travel and keeping busy – but, as forty loomed, the hole that was opening up inside of me became impossible to ignore, and the accompanying sadness became horribly real. I thought that my chance to have a child had passed.

I was beautifully wrong.

To cut a long story short, I met the right man and, at forty-two, I got pregnant.

When we found out, my partner said, 'What would you like to have, a boy or a –'

'Boy,' I answered, before he got a chance to finish his question. I didn't even bother with the indefinite article. Not 'a' boy, just boy. Like a full stop. And the way I said it was like a full stop, too – like a gavel coming down in a courtroom. *Bang.* I remember the surprise on my partner's face, his mouth stuck halfway through the word 'girl'.

'Wow,' he said. 'No hesitation there.'

I think he'd been expecting me to mull it over, then hedge my bets and start waxing lyrical on the delights of both sexes. But he may as well have been asking me if I wanted a glass of red or a glass of chardonnay (it's red, by the way, every time).

It's hard for me to admit this, but I was swayed by the same gender stereotypes that I fight so hard against. That's how crafty and pervasive the damn things are. My automatic thinking was that a boy would be more adventurous and sporty, more likely to dig for worms, read books about lizards, play kick-to-kick and do all the things that I'd done – funnily enough, as a girl. I was living proof that a girl could be as interested in reptiles and sport as a boy, but these rusted-on perceptions and ideas, with centuries of 'validation' behind them, aren't rational. They're kneejerk.

I guess the other part to all this was that I knew that a boy would have fewer obstacles to deal with – less nonsense. That's sad but true. The memories I have of growing up are still fresh; I can still summon up the smells of the school corridors, the boys smothered in Old Spice and girls heavily sprayed with White Linen. And I can still feel the challenges we girls faced – the need to fit in and the peer pressure. While I know that the boys tackled similar emotional obstacle courses, to my young eyes they just seemed to be less intense.

After I gave birth to our son, Francis, my whole life changed. Having a baby liberated me from my past. For the first time in a long time, I was free to think about a future where I wasn't front and centre. This change of emphasis re-energised me and gave me a sense of security that I'd never felt before. It allowed me to think about what was really important to me: things that were more important, it turned out, than my need to be accepted. A weight had been lifted.

Francis has made this book a lot easier to write – and the idea of wanting to fight harder for a better future for him feels right. I feel a responsibility to him that's stronger than my desire to protect myself, and I want to use my privileged position to promote equality.

*

Leading up to the Floyd Mayweather v Manny Pacquiao boxing fight in 2015, there was some public discussion about Mayweather's shocking history of violence against women. Since 2002, five different women have accused Mayweather of domestic violence: he pleaded guilty to two of those incidents, and he was convicted for another, only to have the charges dismissed four years later. In 2010, he received a ninety-day prison sentence for assaulting his ex-girlfriend in front of two of their children.

Mayweather's violent history prompted feminist writer Clementine Ford to tweet in the lead-up to the fight: 'And yes, if you watch the #MayweatherPacquiao fight, you are ACTIVELY complicit in dismissing the seriousness of violence against women.'

I took a different view. I watched the fight *and* condemned Mayweather publicly on radio and social media. By using my platform as a sports journalist, I was able to do more than preach to the converted – something not all feminists have the opportunity to do. As someone 'in sport', I had a chance to discuss the topic of domestic violence with sports followers, a big chunk of whom are men; just as I discussed cricketer Chris Gayle's sexist and demeaning treatment of sports broadcaster Mel McLaughlin to an audience that didn't all see it that way. Regarding that incident, one Twitter follower took the time to message me:

Hi Ange,
My name is Shane and I've just read your article.

Hope you don't mind me messaging you. I just wanted to say something. After the initial interview I did tweet something along the lines of 'everybody take a chill pill he was only having a laugh' or something similar to that. Then, later that night, I read your tweet 'unless you're a woman trying to carve out a career in a male dominated industry, you don't really know what it feels like'. That absolutely struck a chord with me, and I realised right there and then that my original feelings were completely wrong. You're right. I would have zero idea about how that would feel and I couldn't comprehend how Mel felt at that time. I have a wife and two daughters and would hate to think how I would react if that was my daughter on TV. So, all I really wanted to say was thank you for taking the blinkers off my eyes and allowing me to see things from a completely different point of view. Initially I was 'part of the problem', next time I'll definitely think before I tweet.

Regards.

Shane

It's never easy reprogramming the way we think (after a certain age), so to have someone reach out and share their story is really heartening – it's only one male voice, but Shane's understanding that he was 'part of the problem' gives me hope that the conversation is changing in sport as it has in other parts of society.

Since Gillard's Misogyny Speech, the landscape has most definitely changed. You might argue that her speech was a catalyst or just another voice speaking out (or made no difference whatsoever) – it doesn't matter. Over the past few years, something very real has happened. Voices of discontent all over the world, all focused on women's rights, have bubbled and bubbled and grown into something altogether greater. From Rosie Batty to Malala Yousafzai to Patricia Arquette, there's been an explosion of awareness, and all these disparate voices have created an atmosphere that's impossible to ignore. In 2013, even the Australian chief of army, David Morrison, stared down the barrel of a camera and delivered an ultimatum to his troops: treat female soldiers and officers with respect, or get out.

The elephant in the room is no longer just standing there – it's tap-dancing, juggling and belting out show tunes.

A tipping point has been reached.

It was inevitable that at some point the mood created by all these voices would be felt in the sporting community, because things that take place in the wider culture filter down to sport. They may take their time – *really* take their time – but at some point, they start to exert a moral influence. For things to change in sport, for it to become a more level playing field, it must start with strong voices speaking out against sexism and inequality.

On the first Tuesday in November 2015, sport added a new voice to the growing chorus around the world. In one of the most male-dominated professions on earth, something remarkable happened.

The Melbourne Cup is the one sporting event that's watched by all – if you've no interest in sport, if you actually hate sport, if you've no interest in horses, if you come out in a rash when you see polka dots and a pair of jodhpurs, it doesn't matter.

Michelle Payne, riding the 100 to 1 longshot Prince of Penzance, was only the fourth woman jockey ever to ride in the Cup. In the weeks leading up to the race, in all the hours of talk and thousands of words printed about it, she wasn't given a hope in hell – she was barely mentioned. She was invisible.

She won.

The first woman jockey in the 155-year history of the Melbourne Cup to win the race. But Payne's win was more than a feel-good story about a female jockey winning the Cup. Her post-ride interview was as game-changing as her brilliant ride:

> I would like to say that, you know, it's a very male-dominated sport and people think we are not strong enough and all of the rest of it … you know what? It's not all about strength, there is so much more involved, getting the horse into a rhythm, getting the horse to try for you, it's being patient and I'm so glad to win the Melbourne Cup and hopefully, it will help female jockeys from now on to get more of a go. Because, I believe that we sort of don't get enough of a go and hopefully this will help. It's such a chauvinistic sport, a lot of the owners wanted to kick me off. Everyone else can get stuffed [who] think women aren't good enough.

The race that stops a nation also gave it pause for thought. The two words that defined the day were, of course, 'get stuffed' – words that have already gone down in Australian folklore. With those two beautifully simple words, Payne started a conversation about sexism in the horseracing industry.

Michelle Payne has won legions of admirers, and she's also – like all women who refuse to comply with traditional gender roles – managed to ruffle some feathers. And all around the world, feathers continue to be ruffled by women who are speaking out, story after story, headline after headline, protest after protest: women are finding that their voices are, at last, being heard. There is a sense that much of the world has united on this.

When Donald Trump was elected the 45th President of the United States in November 2016, women and men across the globe (and from both sides of the political spectrum) were deeply shocked. Earlier in the campaign, the leaking of his 'grab her by the pussy' comments had sparked a huge outpouring of anger, which many believed signified a fundamental shift in the way we all view this abhorrent talk (and actions). His subsequent narrow win, thanks to the support of an astounding portion of white America, has been interpreted in countless ways. One suggestion is that it's a pushback against the advances being made by women and minorities, advances that many in the US feel are leaving them behind – as the voices supporting equality have become louder, the resistance has grown in equal measure. This possibility presents one of the biggest challenges to equality that we face, but we can be proud that women are continuing to draw strength from one another and becoming more comfortable about speaking out.

*

One of the most common rebuttals when matters of equality are raised is that sexism and inequality are 'first-world problems'. I absolutely agree that war, famine, poverty, natural disasters, human trafficking, child prostitution/pornography, child detention, terrorism in all its forms … all these things, among others, are bigger issues in the grand scheme of things. However, like most people, I'm able to think and care deeply about more than one problem at a time. I can also see the links between sexist jokes and language, the objectification of women, and the more serious crimes of domestic violence, rape, sexual assault and murder. They're all part of a pervasive and deeply rooted problem that we have to care about, because all these things add up – it's like death by a thousand cuts.

Those who can't see the universal footprint of sexism can bluster and bloviate as much as they like, but too many voices have spoken to be dismissed with a roll of the eyes. These aren't just isolated pockets of discontent – these problems cross all socioeconomic and geographical divides, affecting women of all ages, backgrounds and workplaces.

It feels as if there's been, as the French would say, a *prise de conscience*: an awakening. Women all over the world have reached their 'I'm mad as hell and I'm not going to take it anymore' moment. They've had enough of sexual harassment and inequality – at work, in government, in the media, in medicine, in the armed forces, in film, comedy, in the literary world, and in sport. They want to see real change.

But clearly change doesn't happen overnight. There isn't some Fonzie-like click of the fingers and, hey presto everybody, there's change. In 1895, South Australian Premier the Rt Hon Charles Cameron Kingston didn't wake up one morning, mournfully dunk his toast into the top of his soft-boiled egg and think, *You know what? It's time that women should be allowed to vote.* 'Darling, bring me my orange juice ... and another slice of toast. I've had rather a novel idea. I just hope my colleagues like it ...' (Back then, everyone in power spoke as though they'd just wandered out of *Downton Abbey*.) The struggle for women's suffrage in South Australia lasted nine years. During that time, suffragists were labelled the 'shrieking sisterhood' by an unsympathetic media, and they were subjected to public ridicule and vilification. One South Australian Member of Parliament described suffragists as:

> ... disappointed, childless creatures who have missed their maternal vocation; ill-favoured ones who will never get the opportunity of exercising it, the bitter-hearted whose day is past. In any event, if women got the vote it would inevitably lead to the dissolution of marriage and the institution of free love.

Change doesn't have to move with the speed of continental drift. We live in an age where people's opinions can affect real change – and quickly. We have a constant stream of news, facts, opinion, and gossip (and babies, and cats, and dogs) coming at us from a million different sources. Never before has the planet seemed both so small and so connected. It's much easier nowadays to gauge mood, and it's much easier for us to respond to that mood quickly. Whether you love technology or not, there's no disputing its egalitarian nature (all you need is a phone) and its effectiveness in promoting a cause.

Sport is an important part of the feminist movement. But the gender inequities in sport – which are just as (if not more) sweeping as those faced by women in other industries – are sometimes given short shrift by feminists. Women's sport rarely gets a space on feminist news sites, and it has historically been considered too frivolous or (ironically) too masculine to be worth fighting for. I've had this argument with many feminist friends over the years, so I know just how stubborn my opponents on this topic can be: no matter how passionately I put my case, they don't want sport anywhere near their feminism.

But the fact that sport is unapologetically masculine is the very reason why it has a hell of a lot to contribute to feminism. Through sport, feminists can reach men – all types of men. Sport and its traditions, whether good or bad, bring men together, making it a perfect context for those who want to crack open the male code and help to change the attitudes that hold women back across all sectors of society. To brush sport aside because it involves a whole lot of men and balls is counterproductive.

Yes, there are degrees of severity when it comes to feminist fights (rape and genital mutilation are more pressing concerns than World Cup soccer matches on artificial turf), but this isn't about creating must-do lists in order of priority. It's about tackling every issue as best we can, because everything we do, in all walks of life and in all parts of society, forms the moral fabric of our environment. Left ignored, things won't change. We must do the right thing because the right thing matters. And it all adds up.

Since 2015, more women's sport has elbowed its way on to free-to-air TV: most of it not on the main channels, but free-to-air at least. We've seen this with netball, women's AFL, the WBBL and the Matildas (showcased on free-to-air commercial TV for the first time, with all their Olympic qualifiers live on 7Mate). Sponsors are showing more interest too. The Nine Network also introduced a woman, not dressed as a nurse, to *The Footy Show*: former news presenter Rebecca Maddern. It is a step, a belated step, in the right direction. All these changes to the sporting media landscape build enthusiasm and positivity about women's sport, helping to rewrite the story and move the focus from chicken-and-egg conundrums to solutions. And as this happens, more and more people will feel inspired to take up the fight.

As always, I'm optimistic about the future. I spent the bulk of my time as a sports journalist interviewing and writing about men. So many stories about women athletes dropped off the edge of the nightly news bulletin to make way for the 'major sports' – even if that major sport story was a low-list footballer with a chipped toenail. This is finally changing. Younger women journalists don't have to jump through as many hoops to pitch an idea about women's sport. The whiff of the 'token story' is slowly disappearing, and it's being replaced by greater respect and recognition of sportswomen's achievements. Not so long ago that was reserved for Olympic years only, but the opportunities to cover top-class athletes are only going to increase with the new Women's Big Bash League and the introduction of Women's AFL.

Women who work in sport have always been a pretty close bunch with a strong bond, especially in Melbourne. As more women enter the ranks of sports journalism, and more sportswomen take steps towards professionalism, that bond will only get stronger. Importantly, this will empower women in the media to shape their own careers and not feel the need to 'play the game' for the sake of career survival.

Sport must keep listening to the powerful feminist messages that are resonating around the globe. The time is right for the whole sporting community to step up and shake off its ancient tweed, dandruff-dusted jacket, and make a stand against inequality and sexism – the way that some vital parts of the community have been doing for decades.

# 11

# NETBALL

I'm going to play for Australia.

*Angela Pippos (age nine)*

I led a double life when I was seven. Once a week, Mum would drop me off at ballet class. I'd walk to the front entrance of the local scout hall, turn and wave goodbye – then, after waiting for the sound of our Beetle to fade, I'd make a swift exit through the rickety side door. Mission accomplished. Out of sight of the main road, I'd swap my ballet shoes for runners and skip off to the netball courts down the street. I didn't know any of the girls training; they went to my school but were all a few years older than me. And I didn't know the rules. Actually, I didn't know the first thing about netball, but with each clandestine visit my interest grew. Netball drew me in with the same magnetism that drew Miranda through a gap in the rock face while on a school picnic at Hanging Rock: *Angela, Angela …*

This went on for months, until one day I plucked up the

courage to tell my parents about my secret life. To my surprise, they didn't mind at all – they just wanted me to do whatever made me happy. And so, full of excitement, I retired my ballet shoes under the bed and openly began my love affair with netball.

As in all love affairs, there were a few hiccups along the way – like the time I dislocated my finger (the horror, the horror) in the warm-up before an under-14 grand final, and the time I missed out on my club's best and fairest despite being the standout player all season (this would later give me a sharp insight into how Andrew McLeod felt at the 2001 Brownlow). And then there was the time, many years later, when a particularly ferocious opponent followed me back to my car to 'keep it going' (as she followed me, she was cracking her knuckles); *The Dukes of Hazard* aside, I'm not sure anyone in history has ever found their keys, unlocked a door and sped off as fast as I did that day.

For the most part, though, netball reciprocated the enormous love I gave it, and I played (and played) until my legs couldn't keep up with my head. My body, via a series of fierce aches, pains and throbs, raised the white flag … *That's enough, Ange. Perhaps it's time to take up jogging.*

Netball hasn't only been a constant in *my* life; for decades, it's been a strong, unwavering force in the sport industry. In Australia, netball has unequivocally been the sport of choice for women and girls. Over the past two years, other sports have become a lot more visible, presenting women athletes with more choices, but netball has been quietly working away and making slow but steady progress for much longer than that.

For years, netball has waved the flag for women's sport as a whole and kept it in the Australian public's mind, despite constant undermining by the media. Tennis and softball have also helped to achieve this, but netball has the added significance of being culturally important at the grassroots – the constant counterweight to the local footy team. The fact that it's all about women sets it apart from most other sports in Australia: it's the number one female participation sport in the country, with 1.2 million players nationally. (Some men play netball, but not enough for it to be considered a mixed sport.)

In August 2016, I spoke with Australia Diamonds coach Lisa Alexander about netball's place in Australian sport. 'We are everywhere, every city, every country town, every nook and cranny,' she said with maternal pride – and she's right.

What has been debated, though, is how netball fits into the broader push for equality. Some use the fact that netball is a 'women's game' as leverage to argue against gender equality in other sports. The thinking here goes roughly as follows: *Why must we have equality with men in sports that are traditionally male? Why not just stick to men playing men's sport and women playing … netball? Isn't it better for women that we spend more time and resources promoting a sport that's already theirs?*

The first point to make here is that nearly all sports are traditionally male, so this doesn't leave women with much. Aside from netball, which developed out of basketball, and softball, which developed out of baseball, what sports are we left with? Synchronised swimming and rhythmic gymnastics. Whenever men argue that women who want athletic careers should stick to traditionally feminine sports, I wonder how they would feel about being locked into one particular sport, simply because that was the one assigned to their gender? Just because sport and men have been bedfellows since ancient times doesn't mean that we should all obediently accept the cards we've been dealt – apart from anything else, it makes for a dull life for everyone.

It's ludicrous to hold up netball's success as a reason for keeping women out of non-traditional sports. Yes, part of the popularity of netball is built on the attraction of its position as a sport for girls and women. This means that when it comes to attracting talented female athletes, netball has an immediate advantage over team sports such as rugby, soccer, Australian Rules, cricket, basketball and other sports played by both sexes. It doesn't get bogged down in trite comparisons between women and men – their differences in speed, strength, agility and entertainment value; it doesn't have to live in the shade of men's sport and continually spruik its worth and justify its place in Australian society.

On top of that, the women who play netball rarely have to put up with homophobic insults: perverse interest in an athlete's sexual orientation is mostly reserved for women who play traditionally male-dominated sports. Stocky, muscular women competing in any football code are more likely to be mocked as a 'lesbian' (whatever the reality of their sexual orientation) than a similar body type in netball – and more likely to experience discrimination and harassment. For the most part, netball can run its own race.

From my conversations with women in various sports over two decades, it's clear to me that they all share a common goal that's more powerful than the competitive urge to grow their own games. It comes from a shared desire to see more girls and women playing sport for longer. It comes from a shared desire to see more visible female role models in sport. I believe that the success of netball as a participation sport has enhanced the fight for equality across the board, and that's how netball should be viewed – as a bastion of gender equality, not as the basis for an argument that seeks to keep women marginalised in sport.

*

Netball's focus on the bigger picture filters down from the top. When the AFL announced that its women's competition would be played in February/March 2017, journalists were quick to point out that it would 'pose a threat' to the new eight-team National Netball League, which also starts in February, a view fuelled by the AFL's brash claim that it was out to poach the best players from other sports. When I put this to Lisa Alexander, she said:

> I don't believe it is a threat. As an abundance thinker, I believe it will increase the overall chances and role models for more girls and women to participate in any sport they choose. As an educator I believe this is a good and empowering thing for women and girls. I personally think this is another attempt by the sports media to marginalise women in sport, maybe unconsciously, through language such as 'poses a threat'. Finding the non-creative and negative aspects of women in sport. We can all compete and raise each other's standards together, and then increase participation in women's sport.

Alexander's abundance way of thinking continues a fine tradition in netball of women who have challenged the thinking of the day to improve the overall status of female athletes.

Lorna McConchie did it back in 1956. As coach of the first Australian netball team to tour England, which was also the first international team to play England on its home turf, she made it her job to create awareness about her sport. Not only did her team revolutionise the way that netball is played – fast and strong – McConchie made sure the public knew that 'a woman's place' was on the court, although sometimes her message got lost among a preoccupation with the team's sexuality. A month into the tour, the *Daily Herald* reported: 'They're Up on Their Toes, These Girls from Down Under: But They've All Got Boys Back Home.' Well, that's a relief. The last thing we want is a bunch of lesbians gallivanting around England influencing the locals with their wicked ways.

The 1956 tour of England was a big deal – on and off the court. Each player had to contribute £350 towards her expenses (the Holeproof company provided sports socks and hosiery, but not briefs) and, because there was no agreed international code and England was the host, the onus was on the Australians to learn a whole new set of rules. The team was away from home for six months (including travel time) and played sixty-seven matches, only losing three. Remarkably, the test played at Wembley stadium attracted a crowd of 7000 fans, an early sign that elite women's sport was of public interest, as McConchie proudly articulated in her final report: 'Our visit has given a tremendous boost to the game of netball. It has shown that international level contests do a great deal towards bringing the game to the notice of the public.'

But nothing elevated the status of netball in the Australian public's mind quite like the 1991 World Championship final between Australia and New Zealand. Bob Hawke was in the crowd at the Sydney Entertainment Centre – the first Australian prime minister to attend a female sporting event outside an Olympic Games – and there were reported sightings of non-prime-ministerial men glued to television sets across the country. The match was televised live. New Zealand led by a goal at every change; and in the final dramatic minute, defender Roselee Jencke intercepted an attacking pass to secure the win for Australia, 53 to 52. Captain Michelle den Dekker, the hero of my teenage netball playing years, summed up just how significant the victory was: 'It not only took netball, but women's sport, to the next level.' It led to an increase in participation and to the formation of a national netball league in 1996, which became the ANZ Championship in 2008, when the Australian and New Zealand netball leagues merged.

Public awareness of Australian netballers' achievements has been relatively high compared to that of other team sports. This can be attributed to women like Lorna McConchie, Eunice Gill (a former player and administrator over four decades), Joyce Brown (who coached the Australian netball team to three world championship titles in 1975, 1983 and the famous victory in 1991), Michelle den Dekker and Lisa Alexander – who were all unashamedly pro-woman and active in encouraging girls and women to play sport.

However, the unique position that netball finds itself in doesn't protect it from other factors that keep women's sport marginalised. Being so proudly and conspicuously a 'women's sport' is in many ways netball's greatest strength, but in the marketplace this has been its greatest weakness. The sport has consistently struggled to attract sponsors and broadcasting partnerships: it doesn't matter how beautifully the Australians move the ball from one end of the court to the other – they're women. The grassroots popularity of the sport has almost been irrelevant in this context. For a long time, it didn't matter how many loud and fanatical screaming girls were packed into a stadium. Nobody could give netball what its organisers and participants so desperately wanted: a broadcaster that respected the sport and sponsors committed to the product. This was netball's story for twenty years. Whatever it tried, it couldn't translate its popularity among women and girls into commercial gains off the court.

Like other sports played by women, netball players have been susceptible to the usual pressures to sex up in order to attract more media attention and sponsorship. Controversially, the game's administrators went down this path in the 1990s, introducing tight-fitting lycra dresses – much to the unease of Brown and others in the sport who rejected the idea that netball needed to be 'sexier'. And lycra wasn't going to solve the media and sponsorship problems that netball was facing. Attitudes towards women's sport had to change first.

*

Gender bias has constantly stood in netball's way: the men in control of the broadcasting schedules would bury the sport in unfriendly timeslots, and the men in control of the sports pages and bulletins couldn't see past the football codes and cricket. None of this made netball all that enticing to sponsors – nor did its decade on the commercial-free ABC TV.

Jump forward to 2016. Crowds are up, media interest is higher and players are getting recognised after a breakout year for the sport in 2015 – notably the Diamonds' World Cup victory at home (their third straight title) and a thrilling one-goal win by the Queensland Firebirds over the Sydney Swifts in the ANZ Championship decider, during a season that drew 3.3 million page views on Netball Australia's website.

Of course, something bigger was happening throughout women's sport – for the first time in my career, I could sense a cultural shift. And there was another development too, one that would dramatically influence netball in Australia and New Zealand, and severely test relations between the two countries: a split.

Set up in 2008, the trans-Tasman Netball League was the world's premier netball competition, made up of five teams from Australia and five from New Zealand. But the standard of the Australian teams was generally higher, which led to mismatches (eight of the nine championships were won by Australian teams) and ultimately the league's demise. Netball had to do something, not only to better showcase the depth of talent in Australia and even out the competition, but also to maximise its appeal to broadcasters and sponsors. So in 2016, it walked away from the ANZ Championship.

This decision is the circuit-breaker that Australian netball has been crying out for. In its place is a new eight-team national league with five existing franchises (Adelaide Thunderbirds, Melbourne Vixens, NSW Swifts, Queensland Firebirds and West Coast Fever) plus three new additions (a Melbourne-based team owned by the Collingwood Football Club, a Sunshine Coast-based team owned by the Melbourne Storm and a Western Sydney-based team jointly owned by Netball NSW and the GWS Giants). More importantly, the move has delivered the missing piece of the puzzle: a landmark five-year broadcast deal with the Nine Network and Telstra, with two live games to be played on Nine's digital free-to-air channel GEM each Saturday night and the remaining two to be shown on Nine on delay, as well as live on Telstra TV and the Netball Live app.

*Pop* went the champagne corks at Netball Australia headquarters. In announcing the new broadcast agreement, Netball Australia CEO Kate Palmer declared: 'Netball needs to stand up and be counted … we want to play with the big boys.' The deal is big for netball, and potentially a gamechanger for women's sport – which we know must be seen in order to grow.

Alexander warns, 'We're not there yet; we're not in AFL or NRL land.' That's true. We're a long way from that. But what the partnership with the Nine Network shows is that there's been a shift in interest; decision-makers can finally see the potential in a women's sport and the financial returns it could achieve. Eyes have been opened to the untapped pool of sponsors and advertisers who are waiting to be aligned with a fast and exciting sport.

This is hardly a revelation for those in netball, who have spent years lobbying for this kind of attention while most of what they said fell upon deaf ears. Under its previous broadcasting deal, Netball Australia's sponsors effectively paid Network Ten to show the sport on free-to-air television. (All seventy-two games of the ANZ Championship were broadcast on Fox Sports, with the match of the round simulcast live on ONE at noon on Sundays.) This was seen by some as an innovative way to get netball closer to where it needed to be – a good short-term solution to the problem of invisibility – but the deal also had a whiff of desperation and submissiveness about it.

By comparison, the new broadcast arrangement gives netball primetime free-to-air coverage and more money to boost the salary cap, which was previously $270,000 per twelve-player roster. This jumps to a pool of $5.4 million shared among eighty players. At the very least, this will mean semi-professionalism – and for some athletes, it could mean full professionalism.

The trade-off is that the sport will change. Consider what cricket's done over the years to enhance its appeal to broadcasters and bring viewers closer to the action. Microphones near the stumps in the 1980s set off a string of weird and wacky inventions: stump cam, Snickometer, Hawkeye, Hotspot, Spider-cam, microphones attached to players, cameras attached to helmets. Our footy codes stick microphones and cameras wherever and whenever they can; games are played in all sorts of odd timeslots, and Etihad Stadium's roof remains closed in brilliant sunshine to keep the AFL broadcasters happy. The way we view sport has changed immeasurably – this is the world that netball now finds itself in and, like it or not, entertainment-driven rule changes are part of it. Alexander says she's 'very pragmatic when it comes to broadcasting', but the scoring system is sacrosanct:

> I do not wish for the purity of the game to be affected, especially the addition of a 2- point shot. This changes everything you do to prepare a team to win. It will also affect the Diamonds' preparation for international events. Logically it just doesn't sit with me that [the new competition with rule changes] will be any better than the ANZ Championship decider (in 2016) that went to double extra time.

Alexander got her wish – as did the vast majority of netball people. In August 2016, Netball Australia confirmed that there would be no major rule changes for the first season of the national netball league. However, the door has been left open for the 2-point shot to be introduced in year two or three of the revamped league. In announcing Netball Australia's decision, Palmer said: 'So our big job for 2017 isn't to change the game. It's to expose more people to the game; to build that passion around the clubs, create great rivalries, and be very bold in stating that netball is the premier women's code in this country.'

The new league is a victory for players: fringe players and younger players who couldn't find a spot in the ANZ Championship will get a chance to shine; Collingwood players will train on a $500,000 sprung-floor court and breathe rarefied air in the high-altitude room; and girls who aspire to netball greatness won't have to use their imagination – they'll see it live in prime time on free-to-air.

But more needs to happen. Participation has never been the issue for netball and nor has winning titles. The challenge has been increasing the profile of the sport and its players in a country where male football codes and cricket gobble up so much television, radio, print and online coverage. With attitudes changing, netball has a chance to give Australian sport a real shake, but to 'play with the big boys' it must stand proudly female, celebrate its differences to men's sport and stay true to its supporter base, and so must the television coverage. If it manages to do this, who knows what might happen – it may lead women's sport even further into this new golden era.

# 12

---

# OUT OF THE SHADOWS

Someone has to be the best in the world. Why not you?

*Ronda Rousey*

The times are a-changin'. There's more coverage of women's sport (although not nearly enough), and we're starting to hear their stories. Girls have a smorgasbord of sports to choose from, from traditional women's and mixed sports to those that women have infiltrated in recent years. It's not unusual for a sports-loving family to know that Meg Lanning was the first girl to play First XI Associated Public Schools (APS) cricket and the youngest player – male or female – to captain Australia. As for today's role models, you can take your pick from Liz Cambage (basketball), Sam Stosur (tennis), Anna Meares (cycling), Sally Pearson (track and field), Ellyse Perry (cricket and soccer), Laura Geitz (netball), Stephanie Gilmore (surfing), Caitlin Foord (soccer), Karrie Webb (golf), Michelle Payne (racing),

Torah Bright (snowboarding), Jordan Mercer (IronWoman), Jessica Fox (canoeing), Caroline Buchanan (BMX), Kim Crowe (rowing) … the list is super-impressive and endless.

In my experience, most of these women want to be role models. They want to blaze a trail. They understand that their role is greater than their sport, and they embrace it. The reality is that they don't get the same screen-time that male athletes do to allow their status as role models to grow, and while things have improved with the introduction of the Women's Big Bash League (WBBL) and the AFL Women's league, there's much more to do.

Of all the interviews I've done with sportswomen over the years, I can't recall too many where the athlete hasn't wanted to be there – a public appearance with a camera is an opportunity to connect, to tell a story that hasn't been told before. And because they appreciate the opportunity, these women often speak with engaging warmth. I'm not saying that sportsmen don't have these qualities, but our major sports – the footy codes and cricket – get blanket coverage, and this can breed a kind of complacency. How often do we see big sports stars acting bored and contemptuous? The continuous footy news cycle leads to journalists covering anything and everything, and it also leads to players just going into autopilot: 'one week at a time' and 'credit to the boys' whenever a microphone is placed in front of them. Women in sport want recognition, and a lot of them understand the need to actively engage with the media. They want to be celebrated not only because they've worked hard and deserve attention, but also because it encourages girls to follow in their footsteps.

When the AFL announced that rookie umpire Eleni Glouftsis

would officiate the 2016 NAB Challenge game between Essendon and Carlton, it was a big story in the media. She trended nationally all day on Twitter, and TV commentators fussed: a woman was about to umpire a pre-season AFL match for the first time! Should there have been such a big fuss? She'd umpired twelve VFL matches in 2015, so wasn't this just a natural step in her career? Isn't it a bit patronising to single her out – so what if she's a woman?

Well, this is a big deal for a number of reasons. AFL field umpires are all men – and superb athletes in their own right. While running the best part of a half-marathon in two hours, they also need to make game-changing decisions in a split second. Field umpires also need to be strong enough to bounce a football four metres in the air (go down to your local park and try it sometime, it's not as easy as it looks).

Glouftsis' selection as the first woman field umpire at AFL level hasn't happened by chance. As a teenager she was identified through the SANFL umpiring development system as a person with the physical characteristics and decision-making ability to umpire at the highest level. Through guts, determination and hard work, she has got there. This is a big deal because it further weakens the case for those who think that women have no business being involved in the game, let alone controlling the field of play. The sight of Glouftsis running around won't change the backward views of these people, but it will send a strong message to the next generation, a message that women belong in footy.

Girls need to 'see it to be it'. When they see a reflection of themselves, the pathway of what is achievable for women in footy is clear. That's why this is a big deal, and that's why

Glouftsis is the right kind of role model.

During this revolution in women's sport, Australian Rules, soccer and cricket have all started clamouring to be the 'sport of choice' for women and girls, and this new competitive landscape has placed even more importance on sports having visible female role models. The sports that most effectively market their stars get more media attention. That's the way it works. The media loves personalities, especially when they have 'a story' to tell. Thanks to this increased exposure, Ellyse Perry, Meg Lanning, Lisa De Vanna and Daisy Pearce have become known outside of their circle; they're part of the conversation about sport. Isn't it refreshing to hear stories about sports-mad girls who become stars in their own right?

The burgeoning popularity of Collingwood Women's AFL player Moana Hope is a good example of how a team can build its fan base around a talented and much-loved player with a story that strikes at the heart of what it means to be human. Hope gave up footy in 2011 because there was no pathway for women, but she was inspired to make a comeback after watching the first exhibition game between Melbourne and the Western Bulldogs in 2013. She's a brilliant forward, and in 2016 she became the first woman to kick a hundred goals in a Victorian Women's Football League season. Hope is also one of fourteen children and the full-time carer of her disabled sister, Lavinia, whom she describes as her best friend.

Her story is a remarkable one – and only now, with the advent of women's AFL, do we get the chance to hear it.

But the sportswoman who in recent times has become the biggest household name, both here and internationally, is from a very different – and unexpected – sport.

*

Despite my partner's enthusiasm for mixed martial arts (MMA), I've never been that interested in the sport: I just don't get it. I've never been a fan of sweaty men in underpants rolling around a cage trying to – what looks like – mount each other. When I catch him watching the UFC late at night, a typical conversation runs along the lines of:

Me: 'There must be easier ways to get a date?'

Him: 'Go away.'

When my partner was younger (last century), he used to train in martial arts – he took it pretty seriously. Bruce Lee was one of his idols growing up. When the 1970s TV series *Kung Fu* came out, the headmaster at his school had to call an emergency assembly because all hell had broken out during lunchbreak – everyone was trying their head kicks and four-punch combinations on each other. I've heard this story and others like it many, many, many times. But as with most couples that have been together for a long time, part of the unwritten contract between us is the tolerance of stories we've heard six thousand times before.

Every once in a while, he'll try to lecture me on the nuances of MMA: the technical excellence of its competitors, and the mental game that takes place when combatants try to work out each other's flaws. I can see he means it – there's a twinkle in his eyes. He might be recalling a time when he really could do a hundred press-ups without thinking (he now makes noises when he bends down to tie his shoelaces). Who knows? To be honest, I don't usually listen to the specifics. But on one occasion, I did.

I was heavily pregnant at the time and doing some odd things

– I'd stopped drinking tea and had taken up gardening – so I'll put my listening down to an extension of these unusual patterns of behaviour, twinned with my inability to get up quickly from the couch and leave the room. (I'm petite and my baby weighed in at nine pounds two!) And so, pinned to the couch by my own tummy, I heard all about Ronda Rousey. I should check her out, my partner told me, this woman fighter who was tearing through her opponents and causing a stir. The UFC was creating a division for women because of her, and I should keep an eye on it because it would be interesting to see how they went about promoting it.

He had a point, as well as my attention. Here was the toughest, most brutal sport in the world – a sport run by men for men – and here was the largest franchise of the sport, the Ultimate Fighting Championship, the place where every aspiring fighter aims to ply his trade. The most successful and credible organisation in MMA was creating a division for women; the sport was going to do a U-turn on its own set-in-stone stance.

In 2010, the UFC president Dana White famously stood outside his favourite Los Angeles restaurant, Mr Chow, and stated that no woman would ever enter his octagon. This was said with a smile, and with utter conviction – White is famous for not mincing his words. So the turnaround within twelve months makes this story all the more surprising. There was no pressure on White to change his mind; this decision was all of his own making and all down to one woman.

Rousey has fighting in her blood. Her mother, Dr AnnMaria De Mars (PhD in psychology), was the first American to win the World Judo Championships in 1984. Somewhat inevitably, Rousey took up judo at eleven, and by the time she was sixteen she was the number-one ranked American Judoka. She dedicated the next decade of her life to the sport, sacrificing the usual teenage rituals of dating and partying for a life of training. She played by her mother's tough, take-no-prisoners rules – forget about a bowl of porridge, some mornings she was woken up with an armbar (the lesson: constant vigilance). She won a silver medal at the 2007 Judo World Championships and bronze the following year at the Beijing Olympics. But all this success came at a price.

When I spoke to her in October 2015, she told me about her thoughts during that time in her life: 'I wasn't happy doing judo anymore... the process, the training and all of that, I was really miserable, it started only being all about the result and not the process ... so I decided to make a change in my life.' The problem was in finding something that sparked her interest and made use of her exceptional talents. 'I didn't have any work experience, and being really good at throwing people down and breaking their arms doesn't get you much but a cocktail waitressing job in a bad neighbourhood.'

After the Olympics Rousey did bar work, drank, ate fast food, smoked and lived out of her car for a short time before finding her direction. She flirted with the idea of joining the Coast Guard, ignored her mother's advice to go to college and instead settled upon MMA, despite it being a relatively unknown sport with poor exposure for women.

Then Dana White saw Rousey fight in one of the smaller promotions (which had women on the fight card), and he changed his mind about letting women into his octagon. In August 2012, he arranged a meeting with Rousey at Mr Chow, a symbolic gesture in light of his comments there only twelve months earlier.

When they left the restaurant that evening, Rousey was part of the UFC:

> I don't really wake up every morning being like, oh, I'm a pioneer. I wanted a job that wasn't there so I decided to create it for myself ... and every other woman who wanted to do it as well ... I try not to think about things on that grand a scale, so I don't really get crushed under it all.

I was hooked the moment I laid eyes on Rousey. I didn't suddenly become a fan of the sport itself: my interest was cultural. What made her want to do that for a living? How could she do that to another woman? What was her motivation? How did she feel after twisting her opponent's arm to within a millimetre of snapping (and beyond)? These were the questions that went through my head. And why do I find Rousey and other women fighters so fascinating?

The answer – like so many things I find fascinating – lies in society and its conventions. No one in sport turns the 'woman as nurturer' stereotype on its head quite like a woman who steps into a ring or cage to beat her opponent to a pulp. Any woman who ventures into a masculine sport is, to some extent, redefining what it means to be a woman – whether in football, soccer or rugby, these women are demonstrating that they too can be physically strong, assertive and tough – but women fighters don't just break stereotypes, they smash them into smithereens, and that gives them a special place in my rebellious heart. It's why history has largely viewed them as objects of passing curiosity: sideshow acts rather than respected athletes like their male counterparts. That was until the Rousey revolution.

Some argue that because MMA is a relatively niche sport with a short history, this made it easier for Rousey to crash through and take centre stage. But what this argument fails to consider is the uber-masculinity of the sport – she managed to break into what's probably the most testosterone-driven sport of them all.

When I was growing up, the only fighters I knew were men, and they embodied a type of athleticism and toughness that epitomised what it meant to be male: to be tough and feared, to be powerful like Muhammad Ali and Mike Tyson. Women just weren't spoken about in these masculine terms – and the fact that they can be today, the fact that women can be tough and feared (and respected inside the ring) is down to Rousey and the stereotypes she has (literally) knocked out.

The Greeks introduced the sport of pankration into the Olympic Games in 648 BCE – the first recorded form of what would later come to be known as MMA. The sport only had two rules: no biting and no eye gouging. That's how the UFC began too. In the early 1990s, it banned biting and eye gouging, but allowed pretty much everything else: hair pulling, head butting, groin strikes and fish-hooking, to name but a few. In response to criticism, it outlawed these less palatable elements, but the modern version of MMA is still the purest form of one-on-one competition – it's made up of several fighting disciplines, including boxing, Brazilian jiu-jitsu, wrestling, Muay Thai, karate, judo and others.

This is why Rousey is extraordinary, and why comparisons between Rousey and Serena Williams don't always work. Williams is everything Rousey is: powerful, strong, muscular, fiercely competitive and a great sporting role model for girls, and, unsurprisingly, both have been subjected to relentless body shaming. But the one critical difference is that Williams has made it to the top of a sport more associated with femininity. I don't mean this as a dig at her greatness; she's arguably the greatest female player the game has ever seen, and her record (twenty-two Grand Slam singles titles and counting) speaks for itself. But there's something truly remarkable about a woman who smashes all conventions to become the most singular force in the most brutal sport on the planet. It shows that anything really is possible if the desire to change things is there – from both the athlete and the governing body. And it makes a mockery of the Australian media's fixation with the chicken-and-egg theory. There wasn't any interest from the public, sponsors or advertisers for women's divisions to be set up, nor was any interest shown by the mainstream media. The decision to include women in the UFC came from an understanding that women fighters have talent and including half the population in what you do is economically and, whether they thought it or not, morally right.

*

A lot has happened in the world of MMA since that meeting in Los Angeles between White and Rousey. White saw the dollar signs and knew that this was a chance for the UFC to stand out in the market and do what boxing hasn't been able to do with its women fighters: give them a voice and equal billing.

Once the decision was made, there was no messing around. In 2013, the women's bantamweight division was added to the

UFC. The history-making first women's bout to take place (in the previously male-only octagon) was between Ronda Rousey and Liz Carmouche. It was UFC 157, and they were the headline act. In 2013, Rousey and another fighter, Miesha Tate, coached both male and female teams in the UFC reality TV show *The Ultimate Fighter*. In December 2013, the UFC added strawweight to the women's division – a reflection of the successful integration of women into its organisation; in 2014, *The Ultimate Fighter* featured all-female strawweight teams.

In the next seven fights that Rousey took on following UFC 157, she was either the headline act or she shared it. Now in the media conferences before and after each fight, women fighters share the stage with the men. The huge, dramatic promotional banners feature both men and women. As the sport has expanded, so has its coverage on television; and on UFC panel shows, women feature as reporters and hosts.

Rousey became the face of the UFC, the highest-paid athlete – male or female – in the sport, and the most recognisable fighter on the planet. She's more than a household name – she has lucrative sponsorship deals, she appears on billboards all over the world, she's landed parts in Hollywood movies and on all the primetime chat shows, she's been referenced in rap songs, and children in playgrounds across the globe imitate her moves. In 2015, Rousey was a popular choice for Halloween outfits: little girls in judo outfits, furrowing their brows and pulling tough-girl faces as they hit the streets to trick or treat. Rousey is part of the cultural landscape; her name is synonymous with fighting and strength.

Then, in November 2015, Rousey took on Holly Holm in Melbourne. UFC 193 was the first time in combat sports history that women have featured as both the main and co-main events (strawweights Joanna Jedrzejczyk and Valerie Letourneau were the other fighters at the top of the history-making card).

In the lead-up to the event, organisers decided to have some of the women fighters perform open workout sessions in Melbourne's Federation Square. At the time, I was working on a documentary series called *Women Who Fight*, and I decided to film the sessions and the crowd. Lying in bed the night before, I played out the scene in my head – the crowd, girls and women of all ages chanting, 'Ronda, Ronda, Ronda.' I wanted there to be a deep connection between the fans and Rousey, and I wanted to hear how Rousey was an inspirational role model: not just as a fighter, but as a woman unafraid to speak her mind about the stuff that really matters to girls and women in today's society – domestic violence, empowerment, equality and body shaming:

> I didn't have any role models for my body type growing up – I felt like that somehow made me undesirable – is there something wrong with me? I think the only problem is the type of women that are glorified is unhealthy, it's just a very small fraction of the population – I mean some girls actually do look like that but a lot don't – I think that every body type in its healthiest form should be represented in the media in a feminine and desirable way.

For the past few years, I'd been observing 'The Rousey Factor' from afar. In Federation Square that day, I was plonked in the middle of it, immersed in all its vitality and mayhem. It played out much like the version in my head, more Beatlemania than anything I'd encountered before in sport – cries of 'We love you, Ronda!' rang out over the square, and every time Rousey stopped her workout to prepare for her next drill, she gave the crowd a smile and a wave, inciting another round of wild applause.

When it was over, the fans hung around for selfies, and Rousey obliged, slowly working her way down the tangled mass of outstretched arms, mobile phones and beaming smiles. Afterwards, they told me what Rousey meant to them – the way that she could be herself, brash and confident, and redefine (for many) what it means to 'fight like a girl'. And as a campaigner, the way she talked about many issues that male fighters would never address (not because they don't want to but because they're not relevant to them): body image, being your own super-heroine, being independent and not 'a do-nothing bitch'. (This was Rousey's swipe at the kind of woman her mother raised her not to be: 'The kind of chick that tries to be pretty and be taken care of by somebody else.')

Imagine if cricketing great Betty Wilson and other hidden female role models had been given a platform like this to build their public profile and freely express their views about being a woman in sport. Notwithstanding the vernacular, Wilson and Rousey share the same belief: women should be able to choose their own path and not the one scripted for them. Picture, for a moment, if that view had been encouraged to prosper; Australia would look very different today – it probably wouldn't be equal but the conversation about sport wouldn't be so one-sided.

Women-only competitions like the National Netball League and Women's National Basketball League aside, I can't remember ever having been in a sporting crowd where girls and women outnumbered boys and men. Never before had I seen girls worship a sportswoman the way boys worship a sportsman. The natural order of things had been turned upside down. The gathering storm clouds should have been a portent – the gods weren't happy. The only thing that I hadn't visualised in bed the night before was the sight of stupefied male journalists with little interest in the sport thrown off balance by what they'd just witnessed. I left feeling energised and a tiny bit smug.

Two days later, a world-record UFC crowd of 56,214 packed into Etihad Stadium while millions watched around the world on pay-per-view.

\*

Looking at all this, it's blindingly clear that when the UFC decided to bring in women, they were serious about it – this wasn't some half-arsed publicity stunt or tokenistic pink-themed gesture hastily put together by the suits in marketing to placate half the population. This was all-in, money-where-the-mouth is stuff. It was a brave decision to bring women into the male-dominated world of MMA, but this decision has clearly paid off – more evidence that supporting women's sport doesn't have to be about charity or egalitarianism for its own sake. Even the harshest critics of MMA would have to show begrudging respect.

MMA has evolved from being a sport for men to a sport for fighters. I know it's far from perfect: there are concerns about the safety of the sport itself, fighters' pay and the lack of a fighters' union, but that isn't relevant to the point I'm making. Ever since that conversation I had with my partner, I've been keenly watching events unfold, watching as perceptions about women in this sport have been turned on their heads. The speed of the transition from a male-only competition to one that shares its arenas and stadiums with women fighters, gives them equal billing, equal relevance – and in the fight business, this is important – gives women equal 'hype': well, it's incredible. In a short time, Rousey has propelled women's MMA from the obscurity of dark and dingy halls on the edge of town into the bright lights of Vegas.

Women fighters are no longer on the outer, and as tough as it is to make it to the top of this hard sport, now at least there's somewhere to go – or to dream of going. Other fight organisations have had women in their ranks, but the UFC is the largest and most powerful. And that itself sends out a strong message: women fighters belong. Of all the sports to lead the way on getting gender equality right, it seems bizarre to me that it should be the toughest, most brutal sport in the world.

The Rousey versus Holm headline act of UFC 193 provided the sport with its biggest upset yet. After totally dominating the first round, 8 to 1 underdog Holm knocked out Rousey in devastating fashion in the early stages of the second round. The ferocious head kick that felled Rousey drew a collective gasp from the whole of the stadium – in a flash, the seemingly invincible Rousey joined the ranks of the mortal. I don't like violence, but I have to admit, no other sporting event that year left me quite as stunned.

Once in a generation or so, someone explodes onto the scene and shakes things up a bit. By their sheer force of talent and personality, they transcend their chosen sport and become something more. Rousey is a once-in-a-generation type of athlete. She is this generation's Bruce Lee – through his films, he brought martial arts to the masses and through her fighting, she is doing the same.

The combination of her talent, personality and the wholehearted backing of her organisation propelled both her and the UFC into the big time. No matter where Rousey's career goes from here, it won't change the fact that she'll have left her mark on history; she has given legitimacy to her sport and shown us all what equality looks like. With Rousey dethroned, the sport no longer has its iconic queen at the helm, but that doesn't mean momentum has been lost. The UFC threw its weight and support behind Holm – a quieter champion, but no less formidable. MMA did the same for Holm's successor Miesha Tate and current bantamweight champion (as of writing) Amanda Nunes. The template has been set.

The message that women fighters are sending has lost none of it punch since Rousey's toppling as world champion. During Tate's visit to Australia in March 2016, I interviewed the then bantamweight world champion about the rise of women in MMA and what drives her to succeed:

> We're literally fighting for our dreams. You know it could also be taken metaphorically too that you need to fight for what you believe in and nobody should be able to tell you that because you're a female that you shouldn't, couldn't or wouldn't do something. Whenever I heard that it would just motivate me more to prove them wrong.... I'm really pleased with how equally promoted we are in this sport with the UFC and the opportunities we've had. Right next to our male counterparts it's really been no different.

The hard work of elevating the status of women in the sport has been done. Just as Bruce Lee changed the Western perception of the 'weak Asian man', Rousey has forever changed perceptions about women and femininity. However you feel about MMA, for those who are passionate about women's sport, some serious lessons are to be learned here. If the toughest sport in the world can value women as much as men and promote a role model like Rousey, then there should be no excuses for those that don't. This is one stunning example of what a large and powerful organisation can achieve when it's serious about supporting women.

For a long time, I've wished that some of Australia's major sports would be as bold.

# 13

# A LEAGUE OF HER OWN

I would love to see women's participation in this
industry at every level just become the normal thing.
*Peggy O'Neal, Richmond President*

In the lead-up to Ronda Rousey's fight against Holly Holm in 2015, I asked her what advice she would give Australian sportswomen striving for equal respect and recognition. She bluntly replied: 'Take the word "woman" out of it. The fact we are women is obvious. It's not a novelty any more. It doesn't need to be said.'

I would never say this to her face, but I think that Rousey is fundamentally wrong about the path to equality in sport. I love the way that she thinks, and principally she's right, but we're not there yet. In MMA (at least in the UFC franchise), women *are* equal – they compete over the same amount of rounds, they're given equal billing and equal promotion, they have plum hosting roles on television, they've become 'faces' of the sport and are some of its highest earners. In Rousey's mind, that's how you earn respect – you play by the same rules. In Rousey's world, women are at the starting line. But elsewhere, it isn't an even playing field. The reality for most sports is that we're a long way from taking the word 'woman' out of it; in many cases, the word 'woman' has only just arrived on the scene.

Enter the AFL.

Belatedly.

Women have been playing Australian Rules football for a hundred years, but as in cricket, their stories have largely been invisible – sidelined, ignored or forgotten. Records exist from as early as 1917 of a women's football side in Perth, made up of shop assistants from Foy & Gibson – these matches were arranged by a group of retailers to entertain the public and raise money for soldiers, children's homes, hospitals and memorials – and during both world wars, women were called upon to fill in while men were away fighting. It was then up to a few passionate women to keep the game alive until things got more serious with the formation of the Victorian Women's Football League (VWFL) in 1981, followed by other state and territory leagues around Australia. The VWFL began with four teams. It now has fifty-one across seven divisions and a ten-team VFL Women's competition.

When you take into account primary school competitions, secondary school competitions, junior club football and youth girls' club competitions, it all adds up to 355 female teams in Victoria in 2016 – that's a hundred more than there were in 2015. Girls' AFL Auskick is taking off too. In response to growing demand, many centres are running girls-only groups (53,409 girls were involved in Auskick in 2016 out of a national total of 195,719, and numbers are growing annually).

It makes me wonder how my life would have been different if, instead of skipping ballet class to watch netball training, I'd skipped it to watch girls' footy practice at the nearby oval. Would that have been as alluring? Unlike netball, footy wasn't mysterious to me. I'd already clocked up countless hours in the street playing kick-to-kick and many more talking about footy, so watching and then joining a football team would have been a natural progression for me. Mentally and emotionally, at least, I had all the right attributes. I'm not sure how my frame would have gone with bone-crunching tackles in my teenage years, but I would've liked the chance to test my body (and evasive skills). Although I remember the odd sighting of a girl playing in my brother's school competition, the flash of a ponytail in a pack of players, I can't recall any girls clomping around in footy boots. It just wasn't a sport that girls played: it wasn't normal.

So how could I ever have possibly imagined an elite SANFL, VFL or AFL competition for women? It was something that never entered my head as a child – nor at university, or even ten years ago, or even five years ago. I'd heard murmurings, and I knew the women's game was growing – and that trailblazers were driving the early stages of the push – but a national competition felt like a pipedream. Now, I'm happy to have been proven wrong. The fact that there's an eight-team AFL women's competition starting in 2017 is bloody fantastic. And on top of the success of cricket's Women's Big Bash League, it does feel as though women's sport is on the cusp of something special.

*

'There's a revolution going on.'

AFL CEO Gillon McLachlan got straight to the point at Western Bulldogs' vice-president Susan Alberti's 2016 Women in Football Breakfast. The original target date for the start of the AFL Women's competition (AFLW) was 2020 – the fear was that there wouldn't be enough depth in the women's game to kick off any earlier. McLachlan lobbied hard for it to be brought forward to 2017: 'Sometimes you have to be a bit aggressive and bold,' he told the crowd of mostly women, who had come to celebrate the role of women in football. He spoke passionately about the need to get the competition right – all the elements, from the draft rules through to the cut of the uniforms – to make it sustainable and set it up for the next 150 years. He spoke about how he'd been 'running ahead of the Commission', and the importance of establishing a talent pathway well beyond participation. This was an opportunity to revolutionise all aspects of women's involvement, 'an invitation for women to step up in all areas of the game'. And he finished with a bang by asserting that the AFL's decision was as much a moral as a financial one: 'We've provided an opportunity for all talented women … We invested because it's the right thing … it makes business sense'.

It is the right thing to do. But in sport, talking about a women's competition as the right thing to do is itself quite radical. From my experience, equality is often something that decision-makers pay lip service to. The UFC was swift to elevate the status of women fighters after first noticing Rousey, but this was largely driven by financial motives, to exploit a gap in the marketplace. So, to suddenly hear that a sport has taken a moral interest in equality over pure financial savviness is newsworthy. To me, it seems impossible to have a conversation about the ups and downs of women in sport without referencing equality, but I'm not a man who's had every door opened for him. Perhaps in moving the goalposts, the AFL will make other sports consider change in this way – through the eyes of equality and not just numbers.

This view sets me apart from some of my media colleagues. On the historic day that the AFL announced the eight teams that would make up the inaugural women's league, some commentators bleated that the AFL was carrying on as if it had invented women's sport. The default position of some journalists was to suck the joy out of the occasion. Mine – as a battle-weary woman in sport – is to celebrate the victories as they come.

This is a first for the AFL. Women finally have an elite competition of their own; you know, that thing men have had forever. Yes, it should have happened sooner. Yes, soccer's W-League came along first. Yes, rugby league has the Jillaroos. Yes, rugby union has the Wallaroos. Yes, Australia's women's rugby sevens team is the reigning world and Olympic champion; and yes, cricket has the WBBL. All these women have elbowed their way into male-dominated sports, which is great – as is the NRL's plan to establish a domestic women's league by 2021 – but why should one cancel out the other? Life's too short to get bogged down in puerile 'code wars'; to get dragged into playing the 'who discovered women first' game. The announcement of the eight foundation clubs in the national women's league was a significant moment in Australian sporting history. It deserved to be treated as such.

Besides, does it really matter if there was an element of opportunism in McLachlan's decision to bring the timeline forward three years to coincide with the start of a new broadcast rights agreement and keep up with other sports? The important bit is that he acted. He broke the cycle by creating opportunities and pathways for women who play football. He didn't wait for things to happen organically, and we all know how waiting for things to happen organically plays out in a society that undervalues women: power doesn't shift, and things stay the same. Change requires acts of courage – the same acts of courage that are driving the worldwide campaign for gender equality.

Dana White's decision to open the UFC octagon up to women, the establishment of the AFLW and Cricket Australia's decision to start the Women's Big Bash League – when you consider just how hostile the sporting landscape can be towards women, you can see that these are all acts of courage. If things continued the way they always have, footballers, MMA fighters, cricketers and all sportswomen wouldn't get close to reaching professional status, women athletes would remain undervalued and hidden, and things would be the same for the next generation and the one after that. The only way forward is to break with tradition, and if that comes with a sprinkling of opportunism – from head offices down to grants to encourage community clubs to set up girls' football teams – so be it. Surely the end game is more important.

*

You can't have a conversation about the rise of women's football without mentioning Helen Lambert, the founding president of the VWFL; Lisa Hardeman, past player, coach and president of the VWFL; and Debbie Lee, seen by many as the godmother of the women's game. Lee grew up playing football on the street outside her suburban home, sparring with her brothers and neighbours. Despite making a splash in local basketball all the way to the Women's National Basketball League, where she played for the Coburg Cougars between 1987 and 1989, she couldn't shake her passion for football. So she started playing for the East Brunswick Scorpions in 1991.

Two years later, the Scorpions were on the brink of folding. Lee, having caught the football bug, needed to find a way to keep playing. A friend was involved in cricket in Sunshine, and after discovering that the local club would be open to having a women's football team, Lee got some friends together and started one up. In 2000, the club became the St Albans Spurs, where Lee remained a one-club player.

Lee played 304 games over twenty-one years and won the Helen Lambert Medal (the women's Brownlow) five times. She's also a five-time All Australian, five-time state captain and fifteen-time state representative. Impressive as that is, it's what she's achieved off the field that will shape her legacy. As a club president and as president of the Victorian Women's Football League (VWFL), she worked tirelessly to promote women's footy long before it was fashionable to do so. After a stint at the Western Bulldogs as community manager, Lee accepted a similar role at Melbourne Football Club. It's no coincidence that she has worked at the two AFL clubs that have led the push for a national league.

In the lead-up to the inaugural AFLW season, Lee told me that all the years agitating for change were worth it: the setbacks, the pain, the doubters and the detractors were all part of her journey, and they've made her the woman she is today. Her motivation was – and still is – clear:

It goes back to that time when I was a young girl and couldn't tell anyone that I wanted to play footy. I was ashamed and embarrassed. And that's the driver. I didn't want any young girl to feel that way and that's where it comes from. And now these young girls they don't have to worry about it. Your daughter can play footy and be proud of it and that's where we want to come to.

Back in 2007, the seeds were planted for a national women's competition. The AFL's first woman commissioner, Sam Mostyn, took it to the Commission, in tandem with the league's second female commissioner, Linda Dessau. The pair continued to raise it at every Commission meeting until the men around the table warmed to the idea of a women's league. 'It just shows how many years it takes to make men move,' Mostyn told me, reflecting on those difficult early days. Dessau, now governor of Victoria, has similar recollections: 'We arrived in a culture that didn't have many women. It was hard at first. But things started to change. It became easier. That's why you put women in – so that things will change. That, and because a diverse range of talents, people and experiences makes the decision making process stronger.' Despite being the one who got the ball rolling at the top, Mostyn says that the credit must go to the 'unsung heroes (like Lee) who didn't give up'.

In 2008 – the year Victorians celebrated the centenary of women's suffrage – Lee invited Susan Alberti, a well-known businesswoman and philanthropist who was then a board member of the Western Bulldogs, to a VWFL lunch at the Vic Country versus Vic Metro game. The League had received a state government grant of $6000 to stage this sponsors/partners/

supporters lunch – the first sit-down lunch that it had ever held during the season. Alberti spoke at the lunch, and at the end she handed over a cheque for $25,000: money that was used to fund the VWFL's first full-time employee. Alberti's been a strong voice and fierce campaigner for women's football ever since.

The AFL's national female talent search began in earnest in early 2016. Like the organisation itself, it was brash and bold. It made no secret of the fact that it was out to poach the best sportswomen in the land – so it enlisted Daisy Pearce, the 'face' of women's football, to lead the campaign. The plan worked. Fresh from missing out on the Matildas squad for the World Cup, Brianna Davey gave the oblong ball a go, as did Australian cricketer Jess Cameron and Ultimate Frisbee star Catherine Phillips, in a group that also included basketballers and netballers. The testing process involved standing and running vertical jumps, agility, sprinting and the beep test, and the athletes were also given a chance to showcase their skills in kicking, marking, handballing and decision-making. The best from each state were fast-tracked into the state academies.

The AFL's tactics drew the ire of many, including Australian Diamonds coach Lisa Alexander:

I abhor the way the AFL is pitching the league. The patriarchal 'divide and conquer' approach is disrespectful to current players who have spent years developing their skills, it's disrespectful of other sports and it shows a lack of sensitivity. I have a more socialist and abundance view – it's better for society and the community to have girls and women playing a range of sports.

On 15 June 2016, AFL Chairman Mike Fitzpatrick read out the names of the eight successful bidders for a women's licence: Adelaide, the Brisbane Lions, Carlton, Collingwood, Fremantle, Greater Western Sydney, Melbourne and the Western Bulldogs. (St Kilda, West Coast, Geelong, North Melbourne and Richmond have been granted provisional licences for inclusion in a potentially expanded league in 2018.)

The NAB AFL Women's Draft was held in October of that year. I had the honour of hosting the first round, and even as I write this I can feel the nervous energy and excitement that filled the room on that history-making day as 145 players anxiously waited to hear their name called out. They weren't the only nervous ones – I'd met a few of the players while working on my documentary, *League of Her Own*, about the rise of women in Australian Rules.

*

The first season will kick off in February 2017 and will run for eight weeks culminating with the Grand Final in round one of the men's AFL season. When the idea of staging the women's Grand Final before a men's game was first mooted back in 2016, a few blokes, a woman called Gloria and a person named Anonymous were sent scurrying to their laptops to fire off comments to the *Herald Sun*: 'Call it the Dulux Cup because it will be like watching paint dry', 'The game should stand alone and see how many women go and support women – I would suggest none'…

It's no real surprise: as we've seen so many times and across so many sports, women who strive to do more than what's prescribed to their gender are often met with a backlash. In 2008, around the same time as the early rumblings of an AFL women's competition were heard, I came across an article by Patrick McCauley in *Quadrant*, a long-standing magazine of the cultural right that has (in the past at least) been a significant player in the Australian cultural landscape. I can't think of another piece of writing that has better captured the paranoia some people have about women and Australian football. Here are a few excerpts:

> For some years Australian rules football has been in the hands of feminist social engineers who wish to establish equity and social justice in the football community. The Australian Football League has submitted to these demands to change the game significantly. This has been implemented through equal opportunity and affirmative action legislation, and has allowed women to enter male dressing rooms, take up positions as members of football club boards, trainers, boundary umpires and goal umpires, pursue careers as football media commentators and journalists, and make major inroads and major decisions with regard to the future of Australian rules football. The players of the game, however, at its highest level, remain entirely and exclusively men. Even after twenty years or so of positive discrimination, not one AFL team has been able to find one woman good enough to play one game ...

Thinking he was being satirical, I read on:

Although there are many women's football teams, and the AFL sponsors and supports girls' football in schools, the true spectacle and essential attraction of the game requires thirty-six exquisitely fit testosterone-pumped men attempting to subdue each other with speed and skill. Football is men's business – it is quite possibly sacred men's business – and the attempts to feminise it are ideologically driven, nasty and envious attempts at a weird kind of retribution, which could prove absolutely counter-productive ...

Okay. He's not joking:

Feminists have not only demanded that Australian rules footballers 'respect women' and be seen to be respecting women, they have also demanded that 'respect for women' should be defined by them. Women have demanded seats on the boards of football clubs, and other positions of power throughout the AFL under equal opportunity and affirmative action legislation. They have bullied their way into sacred men's sites such as the Long Room at the MCG. Much of the newspaper journalism and media commentary has been taken over by women, and it seems that the behaviour of men in and around the game is a constant and persistent point of contention.

It's compelling stuff, and part of me can't help but construct a backstory for McCauley – one where as an 'exquisitely fit testosterone-pumped' young man he was abducted by a gang of dungaree-wearing Rosie the Riveter clones and forced to memorise *Damned Whores and God's Police* by Anne Summers. Any mistake in his recital resulted in him being beaten with a life-size model of Germaine Greer.

> I suspect that there is a vocal minority of professional feminist activists who pretend to speak for all Australian women, but that there is a silent majority of women who are Australian rules fans who do not agree. Many ordinary Australian women across all age groups are serious supporters of Australian rules football clubs and they are perfectly happy with the game as men's business, in fact they may love the game because it is men's business. They support their teams as if they were tribes to which they belonged, and they suffer the defeats and celebrate the victories as if these were their sons and their family. They see their teams as their champions who will keep the barbarians at bay.

> And on and on he goes ...

> The AFL should return to developing the game of football primarily for the benefit of boys and men and secondarily for the benefit of girls and women. It must certainly cease being developed for the benefit of the small vocal minority of suburban feminists.

Unfortunately for Mr McCauley, things have moved on a lot since he wrote that piece in 2008. His adverse reaction to women in football, like that of Anonymous and any others who share his view, is patently sexist. Australian Football is not 'sacred men's business' – it's a game, and it exists for the enjoyment of anyone who wants to participate in it. The statistics also prove that McCauley's 'vocal minority' is delivering something that an enormous number of the 'silent majority' have wanted for a long time: female football participation has tripled over the past five years, and its television presence is also growing. The women's All-Stars game in September 2016 between Melbourne and the Western Bulldogs, broadcast live on the Seven Network, peaked at 1.05 million viewers and was the highest-rating Saturday night AFL game of the season.

The sexist views quoted above are becoming increasing irrelevant as society evolves into a better, fairer and more vibrant place. More relevant are the views of those who support, love and breathe grassroots footy – who coach, umpire, sit on committees, carve the roast beef and raise much-needed money to improve facilities. People like Terry Logozzo, who's been in contact with me over the past couple of years, sharing his thoughts and observations.

Terry Logozzo embodies everything that's great about community footy: passion, commitment and fair-mindedness – and he's seen how it operates from a few different perspectives, including as an Auskick coordinator and junior coach, and now as a field umpire in the Victorian Amateur Football Association and a committee member of the Parkside Junior Football Club. His three sons play football, and two of them are also field umpires. In 2016, Parkside Junior FC started up under-12 and under-15 girls' teams. With all the focus on the AFL women's competition, Logozzo says that the media is ignoring the cultural change that's also been happening at the community level:

I have spoken to many officials from other grassroots clubs who have started (or aligned to) female teams, and the response has been nearly unanimous. Having female players has been a huge boost to their clubs, culturally, financially, more volunteers, stronger community ties, networking and sponsorship opportunities. It has made clubs much more aware of the importance of good sportsmanship, of their on- and off- ground behaviour, helped to reduce the 'niggle' and swearing, and emphasised the need to always act in an appropriate way towards women. This can be a challenge in a high-testosterone club environment, and where the objectification of women in society/advertising/internet porn has never been so omnipresent. A few men might resent the constant presence of women in clubs, but they would be in the minority.

Of course, not all critics of the women's league are red-faced misogynists; in fact, some are quite the opposite. They argue that it doesn't go far enough, questioning why the competition is only eight weeks long and 'out of season'. Ideally it would be an eighteen-team competition with twenty-three home and away games and a four-week finals series, but we aren't anywhere near that yet. The eight-week format is short, but it's a sustainable option – a first step to what will hopefully become a vibrant and viable league.

About a hundred players are coming out of the VWFL to play in the national competition; if they were to play a regular season, the state league would fall over. A short season allows them to go back to playing at their home clubs. The state league must be kept healthy for the elite competition to grow – only when it grows and becomes stronger can it move away from the pre-season time of year to a proper winter sport for women. The other thing to consider is that if the women's competition had to compete with the men's, it would be completely overshadowed in both public awareness and media coverage. Men in the AFL grab headlines just walking to their letterbox. The only way that the women's league will take off is for it to begin by standing alone.

So, should the women's game have different rules to make it more appealing in the early years, or should its rules be the same as those of men's AFL? The rules elicit an emotional response at the best of times – holding the ball, prior opportunity, deliberate out of bounds, ducking of heads (the amount of my life I've lost arguing about these things doesn't bear thinking about!) – but when you throw gender equality into the mix it gets even more emotional. Is it offensive to women that the inaugural season will feature only sixteen players on the field, a size-4 football (full-size is 5) and fifteen-minute quarters plus time on?

Personally, I don't mind those three modifications, and almost 80 per cent of players surveyed from the All-Stars game in September 2016 supported sixteen-a-side. We've seen entire sports evolve to attract more fans and spectators – rugby, for instance, has a few versions, the most recent incarnation being rugby sevens, a sport that's growing in popularity for women and men. In comparison, these kinds of small adjustments aren't terribly upsetting. They're not unusual, either: in golf, women play off a different tee, in volleyball their net is shorter and in basketball their ball is smaller. These modifications, like those made for AFLW, don't strike at the heart of the game.

If it helps to attract more fans and grow the game, it's a good thing – to me, it's more offensive that there are some sports women can't compete in at all, like the Tour de France and the 1500 metres in the Olympic pool. But there's a fine line between making the game more watchable and making it a second-class version of the real thing. What I don't want to see is the women's game being turned into a giant Petri dish: the go-to place for experimenting with the rules. Those sorts of shenanigans belong in the men's pre-season competition, along with the nine-point goal.

\*

The growth of the women's game and the resulting push for gender equality by the AFL has spilled over into other areas of the game. Dissatisfaction over the AFL's handling of allegations against Richmond's Dustin Martin prompted the League to overhaul its policy covering the game's treatment of women.

In late 2015, Martin was accused of behaving in a threatening and intimidating manner towards a thirty-year-old woman at a Melbourne restaurant. Martin admitted to being intoxicated and said that he had no recollection of the incident. The AFL Integrity Unit started investigating the matter before handing it over to Victoria Police, but the woman decided not to make a statement to police and they eventually dropped their investigation. The AFL also cleared Martin of any serious wrongdoing, but Richmond slapped him with a $5000 suspended fine for being intoxicated and for using obscene language during the altercation. Remarkably, at the time there were no women in the AFL Integrity Unit, which meant that the complainant (and other women wishing to make complaints) was questioned by male investigators, most of them former police officers. In June 2016, the AFL appointed a female investigator to its integrity team.

Sex Discrimination Commissioner and Carlton board member Kate Jenkins (who completed a damning review of sexual harassment and sexism in the Victoria Police), former chief commissioner of Victoria Police Ken Lay and the CEO of Our Watch, Mary Barry, are overseeing the review of the AFL's eleven-year-old Respect and Responsibility Policy, which has no clear framework covering domestic violence, sexual harassment or discrimination. Jenkins says that the complaints process needs modernising: 'Can it be done in a less judicious way where everyone gets a better outcome that's not about victims and villains?' But this review is about more than just player behaviour. Importantly, it will tackle gender equality across the competition – and notably at AFL headquarters, where women struggle to crack the glass ceiling. The advisory group is expected to look at creating reference points for the Australian Football Hall of Fame selection panel, which currently has none when considering players with a history of violence against women.

The AFL is investing heavily in women's football and, in the process, taking a good hard look at itself to make the whole sport more inclusive. Andrew Demetriou, Gillon McLachlan and Mike Fitzpatrick are doing this not because they're the 'suburban feminists' that Patrick McCauley mentioned, but because they know it's the right thing to do.

It has to be asked, though: where are the women making decisions about women's football – or any other parts of the game, for that matter? The first woman to sit on the AFL Executive, Christine Ogg, left in 2012. Three years later, the second woman permanently appointed to the Executive,

Dorothy Hisgrove, resigned. Not long after she left, Liz Lukin joined the Executive as general manager of corporate affairs and communications: continuing the league's unofficial policy of one woman at a time.

In 2016, the woman responsible for creating cultural change around women's and girls' inclusion in football and the AFL resigned. As AFL Victoria's female football development manager for nearly ten years, Chyloe Kurdas established a record number of community-based female teams (more than three hundred) and competitions, and set up an under-18s high performance program for over 450 of Victoria's most promising female footballers. Her work and results have been vital in demonstrating that there's a critical demand from women and girls to play the game, and enough talent and appropriate talent development structures in place to build future talent and support the AFLW.

If the AFL's going to talk a strong game about equality, it must lead by example so that talented women can thrive and stay involved in football.

As it stands, a fifteen-year-old playing Youth Girls can aspire to play like Daisy Pearce, but she'll generally have a male head coach, a male talent manager, a male state female talent manager, a male state talent manager and a male state CEO – and, higher up in the AFL, a male head of female football, a male general manager of game and market development, and a male CEO. Women role models in leadership positions are thin on the ground.

Fortunately, while achieving full professionalism for women footballers may take years, it has begun. Girls will be able to watch Stephanie Chiocci, Katie Brennan and Tayla Harris, and emulate their moves the way I tried to fly like Danny Jenkins.

AFLW doesn't come with a five-year free-to-air broadcast deal like the new national netball league, but with its emphasis on sustainability and viability, it's the right model for other major male-dominated sports played by women – and these sports, more than netball, are the ones that challenge female stereotypes and can really drive sociocultural change. Jenkins says that having a women's team has 'already changed the culture' at Carlton: 'You can't go in all guns blazing – you have to build the supporter base first and the rest will follow.' Aligning women with the AFL's robust brand will do great things for women's sport across the board. Images of women crashing through packs and ferociously tackling one another will change the ways that some people think about women, sport and physicality.

# 14

## THE PRICE OF EQUALITY

Everyone thinks women should be thrilled when we get crumbs, and I want women to have the cake, the icing and the cherry on top too.

*Billie Jean King, March 2016*

Over the past few years, not only have our sportswomen been performing superbly, but something equally (if not more) inspiring happened away from the bright lights of competition – something with far-reaching consequences. Our sportswomen took a stand for equality. No longer prepared to accept second-class status, they found their voices and demanded a better go.

Decades ago, the global push for equality in the 1960s and '70s led to the implementation of laws preventing overt forms of discrimination. For instance, Title IX of the *Education Amendments Act of 1972* is a US federal law that states: 'No person in the United States shall, on the basis of sex, be excluded from participation in, be denied the benefits of, or be subjected to discrimination under any education program or activity receiving federal financial assistance.' Title IX was revolutionary. It's best known for its influence on high school and college sports, making it possible for young women to take the same classes and have the same athletic opportunities as young men. But what it couldn't do on its own was break down gender norms and close the wage gap in sport.

The recent and continuing wave of frustration and anger worldwide is proof that laws alone aren't enough – we have to change hearts and minds to achieve gender equality – and sport is beginning to understand that.

When the Matildas took us on a wild ride all the way to the quarter finals of the 2015 World Cup, they achieved something that no Australian senior football team has ever managed – a win in the knockout stage of the tournament. The one–nil win against Brazil was the moment when the Matildas raised the eyes of the broader public and announced themselves; it was the moment, after years of struggling for recognition, that the Matildas elbowed their way into the mainstream. That was a culmination of years of blood, sweat and tears on and off the pitch. When you're on the road to change, there's often a single moment when it all comes together, and this was it for women's soccer in Australia.

But despite kicking goals on the world stage, the Matildas got nowhere near the same media coverage as the Socceroos, who played with considerable verve and ambition but lost all three of their group matches against Holland, Chile and Spain at the 2014 World Cup. Brihony Tulloch wrote in *Crikey*:

In the past four weeks the Matildas have been mentioned over five hundred times in major metropolitan newspapers across Australia. But between the week before the Men's World Cup started on 12 June last year until it ended on 13 July, the Socceroos were mentioned in the news a grand total of 2597 times. They also graced the front pages of newspapers more than sixty times, with the Matildas lagging far behind.

The rise and rise of the Matildas continued after the World Cup. On International Women's Day in March 2016, they qualified for the Olympics for the first time in twelve years. Their win against Japan (former world champions and the number one team in Asia) in the opening match surprised everyone outside of their inner circle, and it set the tone for the rest of the round robin tournament, which saw them finish on top of their qualifying group for Rio with four wins and a draw in Osaka. And, in further proof of changing times, the Seven Network broadcast the Matildas Olympic qualifiers on free-to-air television.

On the back of their performance in Japan, the Matildas claimed the world number five position in FIFA rankings – Australia's highest ever FIFA ranking in men's or women's soccer. On top of that, for the first time ever, Australia claimed the Asian Football Confederation number-one spot, a position Japan had held since May 2010.

The team that had dutifully been known as the 'Female Socceroos' before 1995 (thank you, Banjo Paterson, for inspiring the name change) has forged its own identity with its attacking style of soccer. That we could talk about the Matildas as medal contenders before the 2016 Rio Olympics shows how far they've come, and despite a heartbreaking penalty shootout to Brazil, they've lost none of their shine.

It's extraordinary to think that not so long ago the team was in disarray. In April 2014, the players called for the removal of their coach, Hesterine de Reus. Many felt disenchanted by her player management style, rigid training methods and strict disciplinary regime. It came to a head at a tournament in Cyprus when the players were told that they weren't allowed time to themselves to leave the team hotel. The Dutchwoman was sacked that same month.

That show of player power was a sign of things to come. In the second half of 2015, the Matildas pushed their demands for a new collective bargaining agreement and boycotted the American tour where they were scheduled to play against the reigning world champions in front of sell-out crowds of more than sixty thousand. Some players broke ranks on the issue, explaining that they wanted to play for their country and worried they may not get another chance. Former captain Melissa Barbieri supported the strike and explained her position this way: 'I can say yes to going to America, no problem, but I'd rather make a stand for the girls ... I'd rather be remembered for standing for something, for being part of change.'

The Matildas and the Football Federation Australia (FFA) came to an agreement in November 2015. Before the pay rise, top players were receiving around $21,000 per annum. In 2016, top tier players in the Matildas earned a base salary of $41,000 a year, while second tier players got $30,000. Match fees are paid on top of that amount – $560 for a standard match, more as they progress through big competitions like the World Cup. The domestic W-League has a salary cap of $150,000 per team with a minimum spend of just $35,000. (Only two teams, the all-conquering Melbourne City and Canberra United, came close to paying the cap in the 2015/16 season.) By way of comparison, the A-League has a salary cap of $2.6 million per team, and clubs must spend at least 90 per cent of the salary cap.

The Matildas should be commended for the fight they showed off the pitch. It sent a loud and unequivocal message to women and girls everywhere that women matter. Pay matters. And it's been heard at the top. The FFA and PFA have formed a joint working party (with input from the nine W-League clubs) to establish a Collective Bargaining Agreement (CBA) for the national league players. And, in October 2016, the W-League inched towards professionalism by stopping the practice of using unpaid amateur players. Amateurs will now receive an allowance in line with male National Youth League and state competitions – between $60 and $150 a week. It's not much, but at least the thinking has changed.

The nation's top netballers took a similar stand to the Matildas back in 2005 when the Australian Netball Players' Association joined with the Australian Workers' Union to secure better pay and conditions, but the Matildas took their collective action a step further. The fight for a decent income was the headline act, but more powerful than that was their rejection of the notion that women should be grateful that they get the opportunity to play elite sport just 'for the love of it' – a mantra so ingrained that athletes themselves believe and perpetuate it.

*

Tennis is one of the few global sports that pays everyone the same amount in major tournaments. Throughout sporting history, it's hard to think of a better example of collective action for pay parity than the Billie Jean King-led campaign in the 1970s.

At twelve, King decided that she wanted to fight for equal rights for girls and women. When she won the Italian Open in 1970, her prize was $600. The men's winner, Ilie Nastase, took home nearly six times that – $3500. In the same year, King and eight other female tennis players decided to boycott the peak body for professional tennis, the International Lawn Tennis Association, after it started scrapping women's tournaments from previously combined events. Women across the sport were also paid significantly less prize money than men.

Following on from this, King founded the Women's Tennis Association (WTA) in 1973 and refused to play the US Open unless women received equal prize money. Her tactics worked. The US Open became the first major tournament to award equal prize money to its male and female players, and the other majors followed suit. In 2007, Wimbledon, the oldest tennis tournament in the sport's history, was the last to offer equal prize money to women competitors – a staggering thirty-seven years after the original nine women made a stand.

Tennis's case for equal pay has been strengthened by a few inbuilt advantages that other sports don't have. Firstly, all participants compete on the same stage at the same tournament. This, in the minds of many – not all – eliminates any whiff of second-class status, and with it the programmed response of paying them less. Still, pay parity has not been achieved at all events. What's clear-cut, however, is that the strides in gender equality that have been made so far couldn't have been achieved if women in tennis hadn't disrupted business as usual, organising together and boycotting tournaments until they were paid fairly. Visible, significant collective action was crucial for women's tennis to grow – and, perhaps contrary to what many argued at the time, it also drew attention to and encouraged investment in the game, the results of which we see today.

In 2014, the women's tour signed a game-changing deal. Digital sports content and media group Perform agreed to pay $525 million for rights to singles matches over ten years from 2017 to 2026, the largest in the history of women's sports. The agreement gave rise to WTA Media, the tour's dedicated media arm, which will produce all two thousand main-draw matches on the women's tour, live.

The actions of King and others in the 1970s gave players a voice, more money and a sense of self-worth, and were instrumental in building the tour into the high-profile and competitive scene it is today. But despite there being equal prize money in tennis in all four majors since 2007 – and combined Masters events such as Indian Wells and Miami – the debate about women's pay just doesn't go away.

In 2016, former Indian Wells tournament CEO Raymond Moore got things going again when he said that the women's WTA tour 'ride on the coat tails of the men'. The 69-year-old South African former player went on to say, 'If I was a lady player, I would go down every night on my knees and thank god that Roger Federer and Rafa Nadal were born, because they have carried this sport. They really have.' Moore later apologised for the 'erroneous' remarks, which he made just prior to the Indian Wells women's final between Serena Williams and Victoria Azarenka, and he's since resigned from his position. Williams was quick to condemn him, saying that women 'shouldn't have to drop to our knees at any point', while Billie Jean King tweeted: 'Disappointed in Raymond Moore comments. He is wrong on so many levels. Every player, especially the top players, contribute to our success.'

Novak Djokovic also weighed in with his take that male tennis players have a right to demand higher pay because the prize money should be 'fairly distributed' based on 'who attracts more attention, spectators and who sells more tickets'. I like Djokovic a lot: I like the way he plays, I like his demeanour and I especially like the fact that he cares for disadvantaged children. In setting up the Novak Djokovic Foundation (which invests in early childhood development programs in his home of Serbia and internationally), he's used his influence to make a real difference. But on the issue of equal pay in tennis, he's misguided: he should feel proud that he belongs to a sport that truly believes in the principle of equal pay for equal work; for most sports, parity is still a goal.

Overall, the crowds for an average match are roughly the same at men's and women's majors, and the TV ratings are also roughly equal. Australian tennis fans are no less likely to watch a Sam Stosur match than one featuring Bernard Tomic. It's true that men's tennis has enjoyed a recent golden age with Federer, Nadal, Djokovic and Murray perched at the top, and this affects television audiences for finals, but red-hot rivalries and star power in tennis are cyclical, and they're also a feature of the women's game: we've had Martina Navratilova v Chris Evert, Steffi Graf v Monica Seles, and Serena Williams is a drawcard all by herself because she is Serena Williams.

From another angle, those who huff and puff about equal pay in tennis often do so because women play fewer sets than men, and by their assertion this should mean less money – as if a major tennis tournament was a shift at McDonald's. Those who argue this point don't understand (or choose to ignore) the principle of equal pay for competing on the same stage with the same crowds and TV. The discussion over how many sets women should play in slams is a legitimate debate – the International Tennis Foundation, which runs the Grand Slam events, dictates that men play best-of-five sets and women play best-of-three, and has consistently ignored the WTA's suggestion that women players would be willing and able to play five sets. The reasons floated for keeping the current structure tend to revolve around scheduling, along with an audience preference for shorter matches. It's a sporting argument and it shouldn't get dragged into a conversation about equal pay. But invariably it does.

The path to the top for male and female players involves a similar amount of practice hours, blisters, forehands, backhands and dummy spits. No matter how you dice it, in making it as professional players, women work just as hard as men – and when it comes down to it, prize money is for winning, not for how long it takes to convert match point. The Australian cricket team doesn't get paid less for winning a Test in three days rather than five; a boxer doesn't get paid less for a first-round knockout; a men's tennis player doesn't get paid less for winning (or losing) a match in three sets rather than five. If the number of hours competing was the main factor in determining how much sportspeople were paid, then women who play soccer in the W-League or represent Australia in cricket would be earning just as much as their male counterparts. Professional tennis players get paid because they entertain masses of people (and attract advertising dollars). It's the same for all professional sportspeople – the duration of the contest doesn't matter.

Responding to Djokovic, Andy Murray rightly pointed out that the level of interest varies depending on the match. In 2015, the US Open women's tournament sold out more quickly than the men's. In 2013 and 2014, the women's US Open final amassed higher TV ratings than the men's. In 2005, the Wimbledon final between Venus Williams and Lindsay Davenport drew one million more viewers than the men's final between Roger Federer and Andy Roddick.

*

There are similarities between the Matildas and Australia's women's cricket team, the Southern Stars: another high-performing, underpaid women's team. As the dominant summer sport in Australia, men's cricket has enjoyed all the trappings – extensive media coverage, juicy contracts, rusted-on sponsors and glorification. Up until quite recently, women who chose to play cricket were thought to have simply lost their bearings on the way to a netball court. They were relatively unknown, their achievements hidden – and they certainly didn't make any money from the sport or attract commercial interest. But in the past few years, women's cricket has made up ground and is now enjoying a surge in popularity, thanks largely to the success of the T20 format, the achievements of the Southern Stars, and the appeal of Ellyse Perry and Meg Lanning. The queue of kids lining up for autographs is sometimes as long for Perry as it is for any player in the men's team.

2015 was a defining year for Captain Lanning and the Southern Stars. The team regained the Ashes, their first series win in England in fourteen years. Lanning smashed a heap of runs, and even the cricket bible *Wisden* took notice, including a women's award for the first time in 150 years, with Lanning crowned inaugural Leading Woman Cricketer in the World. By October 2015, the Stars were ranked first in all forms of women's international cricket. It's not that they hadn't won anything before (they'd won six World Cups and more World T20 titles than any other nation), but the team's earlier success didn't get the recognition it deserved.

Owing to the introduction of the Women's Big Bash League (WBBL) in 2015, women's cricket is now (occasionally) on free-to-air television, and it's even found its way onto Network Ten's main channel. When the season one Melbourne Derby between the Stars and Renegades was moved from ONE HD to the main channel, TV audiences peaked at 404,000 and 13,000 people attended the game. In season two, the network went a step further – the Stars v Thunder game in December 2016 was the first standalone (as opposed to curtain-raiser) women's sporting match in primetime on a commercial free-to-air TV network's main channel.

Sponsors are also showing more interest in women's cricket. In October 2016, the NSW Breakers in the WBBL became the country's first fully professional domestic women's sporting team, thanks to a deal with naming-rights partner Lendlease.

This is what change looks like. The WBBL demonstrates that Cricket Australia is serious about making up for lost time. It's an exciting era, not only for the talented women who play the sport, but also for the army of girls who slop on the sunscreen and pull on the pads after school and on weekends to carve their names into suburban folklore. Whether, as Cricket Australia hopes, cricket will become the number-one team sport for girls and women remains to be seen, but things are heading in the right direction. People are talking about the WBBL – I can now start and finish a conversation about women's cricket at a party without the person I'm talking to looking at me as if I've just launched into my take on quantum mechanics when applied to everyday household objects.

The wage gap is still eye-popping stuff, but inroads have been made since 2013 when Cricket Australia introduced central contracts for women that allowed some Australian players to turn professional (England followed in 2014; India in 2015). Cricket Australia also introduced contracts for state players, so cricketers who play in the 50-over Women's National Cricket League (WNCL) now get a small retainer. After two wage increases, in 2016 Australia's elite female cricketers became the best paid of any women's sporting team in the country. Maximum retainers for the Southern Stars rose, from $49,000 to $65,000, with another $15,000 on top for those players contracted to the Women's Big Bash. WNCL payments also rose, from $7000 to $11,000, meaning that Australia's best domestic female cricketers (WBBL and WNCL combined) now earn $26,000 a season.

*

Equal pay isn't alien to Australian sport outside of tennis. Aerial skiing has always had equal pay, while surfing and BMX followed suit in 2015. And before you dismiss these sports as peripheral, there's also the inspiring case of hockey in Australia, where there's no contractual difference between players of different genders.

In the words of Hockey Australia CEO Cam Vale: 'We treat our athletes as athletes. Whether you're a Kookaburra or a Hockeyroo, when it comes to basic terms and principles in how we remunerate our athletes it's exactly the same.'

But it doesn't stop there. The men currently receive more funding from the Australian Sports Commission (a success-incentivised funding model, not gender-based), so Hockey Australia tips in extra cash to create gender parity.

> One of our key strategies as a board and as a CEO, is to help bridge that gap by using more of our commercial income disproportionately to fund women's programs ... so as far as program funding goes we are always going to fund the programs as close to the other one so we have as equal a chance to have success across both ... A big part of the difference between us and other sports is that we can truly say, hand on heart, we try to win both [men and women] I think it's certainly not the common thread [in other sports] ... It's just core business, standard business for us ... It's ingrained in what we do ...

Hockey's commitment to equality exposes the failings of other sports even more. It's a good thing that the government and the ASC can sometimes step in to keep them in line.

From 2016, major Australian sporting organisations have been expected to provide the same overseas travel standards for all athletes if they want to continue to receive millions of dollars in government funding. Federal Sports Minister Sussan Ley and Australian Sports Commission (ASC) chairman John Wylie wrote to the thirty top-funded organisations, setting out their expectations for change. The letter reads: 'In 2016, we can think of no defensible reason why male and female athletes should travel in different classes or stay in different standard accommodation when attending major international sporting events.'

I just hope that the federal government and the ASC continue to work together to drive meaningful change in other areas where inequality is more deeply felt: access to facilities, unequal pay, participation rates and the lack of women on sporting boards.

\*

When the AFL first announced its underwhelming pay proposal for its women's competition, in September 2016, Collingwood marquee player Moana Hope tried to deflect attention from the ensuing controversy:

> I'm just blessed to pull on an AFL jersey ... The pay is exciting, but right now I get to play AFL. There are generations of girls coming through who are going to be able to fulfil their dreams, and in years to come I'm sure that [pay] will be addressed. When we are around each other all we are talking about is football [not pay].

As pure, honest (and enduring) as that sentiment is, playing for the love of the game and the jumper only reinforces the subordination of women in sport. The Matildas may have put a serious dent in the 'women, sport, love' nexus – but, as we know, it takes time to undo traditions.

Most women athletes' pay still doesn't come close to the astronomical figures paid to the men who play their sports, and realistically it won't any time soon. So as noble as the fight for equal pay is – and it should always be what we aspire to in the long run – right now it has to be about *better* pay. A starting point for that is a fairer base salary so that women have enough money to live while dedicating themselves to their sport. The Matildas still aren't paid a fair salary, but by taking a public stand they have earned respect, that feeling of being treated as legitimate elite athletes and not as appendages to the men's team – not 'Female Socceroos'. This is one of the main reasons why the fight for better pay was worth it: respect from the FFA (no matter how late and how small) and from the sporting public is now being reflected on the park. It's all a far cry from the nude calendar of 2000.

Fighting for equal pay also has to be about investing in grassroots and building a bigger audience so that women athletes can command a bigger slice of the pie. To do that, attitudes must change first. Constant comparisons to what men earn are pretty much useless, apart from reminding us of just how dreadfully lopsided the whole game is for women. It's hard to think of another industry so skewed in favour of men from the day they're born.

Even without comparing the AFL salaries of men and women, the AFLW wages look very light. Under the AFL's initial proposal, most of the two hundred players stood to earn $5000 for a 22-week contract, including superannuation but excluding private health cover. (Marquee players were in line to receive $25,000, and high draft picks and special priority selections $10,000). The AFL justified these low figures with the narrative that the 'journey has begun for women' – although, interestingly, young men beginning their journey as AFL rookies in 2016 earned a base wage of $57,100.

In November 2016, after months of negotiations between the AFL and the AFL Players' Association (AFLPA), a new pay deal was struck. Under the two-year agreement, marquee players will now earn $27,000, priority players $12,000 and the remaining players on the list $8500. Players will still have to pay for private health insurance, but the AFL will cover: footy boots and runners, a travel allowance when playing interstate, income protection insurance, out-of-pocket medical expenses for fifty-two weeks post-contract and a carers allowance for players travelling interstate with a child under twelve months old.

The new deal will make the athletes feel a little more 'semi-professional', but has the journey for women really 'just begun'? If we're to characterise a woman's worth by her journey (or lack thereof), we need to consider the whole journey – not just the final leg.

Think about the journey that most women who play football have been on. In the early years they were repeatedly told that they couldn't play, and those who did shun convention were forced to play in boys' teams, use boys' change rooms, and wear leftover uniforms made for boys that were so large and gaping you could smuggle two extra players onto the field. At fourteen they were told to quit because girls weren't allowed to play in boys' teams from that age. The really determined ones found the path again at eighteen, but four years out of the game is detrimental to anyone's career. The women who managed to make it that far had a hard time getting access to training facilities, playing grounds and change rooms that were gender-appropriate. They had to fight tooth and nail to even borrow a football to train with; they were given the last-choice coach and ridiculed for playing a masculine sport. 'No one wanted to be associated with us,' a former Melbourne University woman footballer told me. Even the curator of the ground offered up his opinion, telling them to focus on their studies and social life, not footy.

This is a typical journey for a woman with a passion for Australian Rules. The AFLW 'class of 2017' got to this point on their own – with society firmly against them. They stuck with the code despite the code offering no clear pathway. So not only are they strong role models because of the way they play the game, but they're also strong role models for showing what you can achieve when you stare convention in the face and crash through. Furthermore, they bring so much goodwill to a game that's had more than its share of off-field drama. Every athlete should feel valued by their sport.

A few nights after announcing the pay proposal, the AFL staged the All-Stars match between the Western Bulldogs and Melbourne at the Whitten Oval – the last in a series of exhibition games between the two trail-blazing clubs. I went along in my role as a documentary-maker; I'd had every reason to believe that the game was going to be a success, and the affirmation of this belief couldn't have been any more complete.

We set up on the boundary line just as Susan Alberti was making her way to her seat in the grandstand. Through the lens I watched her ascent, replaying in my head a conversation we'd had an hour before while waiting for the team bus to arrive. Alberti insisted on greeting every one of 'her players' as they disembarked from the bus. She talked through the range of her emotions: joy, pride, exhilaration, and sadness for those players who'd be leaving the Bulldogs to join other clubs after the match. While all this was running through my head, my eyes still on her, the most amazing thing happened – the crowd spontaneously gave her a standing ovation. It was a special night.

Free-flowing with few stoppages, the game spoke for itself. The feeling around the ground transcended club allegiance; we were all witness to something much bigger, something that would change the game forever. A new game had announced itself, and we were all on the same side – football by and for women.

In the winning rooms afterwards, where the players sang 'Daughters of the West', I stood arm in arm with sports journalist Sam Lane. We hugged each other, saying, 'We've made it, we've finally made it.'

As I mentioned earlier – and it bears repeating – the free-to-air telecast drew a peak audience of 1.05 million viewers on Channel Seven and 7Mate. It had an average television audience of 387,000 in Melbourne, making it the highest-rating Saturday night game of the year. No matter which way you look at it, the women have worked hard for their $8500.

At least the AFLW has prompted pay increases for other Australian sportswomen: there's no doubt that netball's record pay deal, announced in September 2016, was in response to the AFL moving in on its territory. Under the new netball CBA, the average salary for the eighty national league netballers will rise from $40,000 to $67,500. The deal also includes breakthrough conditions for netballers – clubs will pay for children under twelve months old and a carer to travel to games with players, along with private health insurance and income protection for up to two years in the event of injury or pregnancy. It's a far cry from the days when teams would travel with their own microwave to save on food costs, and strapping tape was included as an incentive in a player's contract.

Former Australian Diamond and Melbourne Vixens captain Bianca Chatfield negotiated the deal in her role as director of the Australian Netball Players' Association. In her *Herald Sun* column at the time of the announcement, she questioned why any netballer would cross over to the AFLW:

> Yes, some netballers might make the change, but they won't be our elite players. They will be the ones who already know they aren't good enough to play for Australia. And that's okay. It's not a competition between the two sports. We should be celebrating that women's sport is being recognised now as a main player.

Chatfield is right. In what's been described as 'the new battleground in women's sport', netball, AFL, cricket and soccer are fighting for players in the semi-professional arena – and for the hearts and minds of girls (and their parents) across Australia. If one sport can push another to try harder, it's a good thing. It's the opportunity versus opportunism debate, and once again, I have no problem if opportunism presents itself on the way to a better outcome for women and girls in sport. The end result that I want is gender equality in sport – and if a sport fast-tracks its preparations to keep up with other sports, then so be it.

\*

Australian sportswomen know how to win. In the past two years, we've seen Australian women win the Netball World Cup again, regain the Ashes, beat Brazil's soccer greats – and create history by winning the first women's rugby seven's Olympic gold medal.

Four years ago, the rugby seven's team didn't even exist. Now they're world champions and Olympic gold medallists. The team's motto for the Rio Olympics was 'ROAR': Respect, Olympic dream, Accountability and Rough bitches. They were brought together (after a series of open trials and targeted recruiting) from a range of different sports: touch football, WNBL, athletics, rugby league and rugby. The twenty-player squad is also fully professional, and they train alongside the Australian men's team and the Manly Sea Eagles in the NRL. They have a full-time staff of seven, with coaches, manager, strength and conditioning staff, and a medical team – all this in the space of four years, because the Australian Rugby Union had the desire and will to make it happen.

In Rio, Kim Brennan won gold in the single sculls, while Chloe Esposito won gold in the modern pentathlon; Michelle Payne won the Melbourne Cup; Anna Meares cycled her way into history with her eleventh world track title and added a Rio bronze to become the most decorated Australian cyclist in Olympic history; canoeist Jessica Fox became the first woman to win three consecutive world titles in the C1 class, as well as a bronze in Rio; Stephanie Gilmore won her sixth world surfing title, and Tyler Wright won her first. All of these athletes have, to varying degrees, elbowed their way into the public's consciousness through world-class performances.

The next step on the road to equality is for sportswomen everywhere to become firmly embedded in the national consciousness, so that ability rather than gender is the talking point. It's not a pipedream: in November 2014, the grim weather didn't deter a record crowd of 46,000 turning out at Wembley to watch England take on Germany in a women's football friendly. It was a watershed moment in that country, with the game televised live on the BBC. For the first time, a generation of girls saw the women's team treated the same as the men's, and not just on the pitch. Everything about the experience was uplifting: the excited faces of girls in the crowd who proudly wore their full club kits; young men chanting 'Eng-er-land' with as much zeal for the women as they would for the men – even the advertisement in the program for a brand of tyres showed a girl in her football kit in the back seat of the car. Never before had the sport been subverted in this way.

Performances and pay deals have kick-started momentum and got sport fans talking, not only about women in sport, but about gender issues and inequality in general. There's still a hardcore element that will never see the virtues of women's sport, and no amount of world titles and gold will change the way they think. But as vocal and angry as they can be, in the grand scheme of things, they're not going to stop the momentum.

One of the challenges for women's sport is to keep this momentum going, to build on this success. Winning will help this, of course it will – but as beautiful as it is to win a World Cup or Olympic gold, it won't solve all the problems.

It takes more than winning to reduce the pay gap. And it takes more than winning to change sexist attitudes: Karrie Webb has won seven majors, more than any Australian golfer, but open up the discussion about who is Australia's greatest golfer, and you'll hear the names Peter Thompson, Greg Norman, Steve Elkington, Geoff Ogilvy, Ian Baker-Finch, Adam Scott and Jason Day roll effortlessly off the tongue before a lone voice throws in Webb's name. And that inevitably sends the conversation down the 'Yeah, but that's women's golf,' 'They play off a different tee,' 'The competition isn't as good' path.

You can cut and paste retired basketball champion Lauren Jackson's name into that argument. And surfer Layne Beachley's too.

But what winning does is help us see our women athletes for what they are. Damn fine athletes. And that's a damn fine launching pad to a brighter future for the next generation of sportswomen.

# 15

# MAKING OURSELVES HEARD

Shrill:
Noun (in sing)
a shrill sound or cry: *the rising shrill of women's voices.*

Grating:
Adjective
Sounding harsh and unpleasant: *her high, grating voice.*

Nagging:
Adjective
(Of a person) Constantly harassing someone to do
something: *a nagging wife.*

Oxford Dictionary

As a woman advocating for women in sport, I'm lumbered with
another stereotype on top of all the usual ones. When I highlight

the disparities on and off the field, I'm labelled a 'whinger'. Any woman in sport who bemoans the lack of equality gets that label.

This is a bit rich. After all, when it comes to whinging, men are more than capable of holding their own. Kenny Dalglish moaned about the balls being 'too bouncy' after Newcastle lost to lowly Stevenage in the FA Cup; Sri Lanka moaned about tight-fitting clothes after losing the ICC Champions final to Pakistan; Mervyn King moaned about the air conditioning after losing to Raymond van Barneveld in the semi-finals of the 2003 Darts World Championship; Mick Malthouse moaned about everything; Lance Armstrong moaned about being persecuted by the non-believers; and my all-time favourite, stadium manager John Turner moaned about the boardroom being haunted by the ghost of Lord Nelson after Blackpool gave up a two-goal lead against Bradford in the 1996 play-offs ... and on and on and on.

Legions of world-class whingers gripe and moan their way through their whole sporting careers. When it comes to women being called 'whingers' when we dare to complain about the treatment that we receive in sport, the words 'pot', 'kettle' and 'black' spring to mind.

We're seen as whingers when we draw attention to the fact that women feature in only 7 per cent of sports programming in Australia; that only 28 per cent of board directors in national sports organisations are women; that there are no female change rooms at the MCG; that they don't make Matildas' jerseys for fans; that Western Bulldogs' Vice-President Susan Alberti had to step in and sponsor Australia's fastest woman, Melissa Breen, because she wasn't receiving any funding from Athletics Australia.

Pointing out what's wrong with this tweet by the *Chicago Tribune* made us whingers: 'Wife of a Bears' lineman wins a bronze medal today in Rio Olympics.' Corey Cogdell had won bronze in the women's trap shooting. Same goes for this one by the *San Jose Mercury News*: 'Olympics: Michael Phelps shares historic night with African-American.' Simone Manuel became the first African-American woman to win an individual Olympic swimming gold after she tied with Canada's Penny Oleksiak in the 100-metre freestyle final.

I don't bang on about these things just because I love the sound of my own voice; I draw attention to these glaring inadequacies because I want to improve the situation. Voices need to be heard, and the girls and women who play sport often don't feel comfortable raising these matters. Daisy Pearce, the number one draft pick for Melbourne in the AFL's 2013 Exhibition Series women's draft, sums up the feelings of many women athletes:

> You don't really complain, but that's probably because that's all we've really known and you just make do with what you've got ... I'm always a bit hesitant to complain about facilities and the things that we do have wrong, because I know that as a female I'm very lucky to even have the opportunity to run out there on the football field every weekend.

While I understand where Pearce is coming from – as I've already admitted, I bit my tongue for most of my career as a sports journalist – things aren't going to change without pressure and agitation. Releasing disturbing data is all part of the process of getting to a better and fairer place. Recognising the problem, how deeply it's rooted and how far it's spread is the first step – only then can positive and pragmatic solutions be discussed and put into place. This isn't whinging: this is what it sounds like to be doing something about a problem. A serial whinger – and women's sport has them, just like every other part of society – moans without a plan, without offering up any solutions.

Instead of pigeonholing advocates of gender equality in sport as whingers who take perverse delight in listing one depressing set of numbers after another, critics should join in the conversation about solutions.

*

Women on Boards Australia Executive Director Claire Braund believes real change comes from giving women more seats on sporting boards. In October 2014, she told the Asia Pacific World Sport and Women conference, 'Fewer female voices at the top level in sport will result in female athletes remaining second-class citizens in terms of media coverage, funding and salaries.' According to the International Working Group on Women in Sport, of the fifty chief executives of national sporting organisations in Australia, nine are female. That 18 per cent figure – along with the fact that nearly 30 per cent of the sporting board members in Australia are female – is one of the best in the world.

But does putting women on sporting boards actually change the culture of an organisation? Johanna Adriaanse, co-chair of the International Working Group on Women in Sport, says yes, but that it has to be more than a token effort: 'One female board member is token, two is a minority, three starts to change the conversation. A minimum of three is a critical mass of women that can influence the culture of the organisation.'

From my point of view, it's pretty simple. Women bring a fresh perspective. They bring a different voice, a different energy, a different sensibility and different life experience. And diversity of all kinds on boards makes good business sense – it reflects the real world. A board made up of divergent backgrounds means that the same idea can be tackled in many ways, and this can lead to healthy debate, which in turn can lead to better decisions. It also sets an example that hopefully has a trickle-down effect within the sport or organisation. A roomful of men with the same story (all wearing the same blue tie) doesn't allow for this. In the words of Managing Director of the International Monetary Fund Christine Lagarde, it instead leads to a situation where men 'show how hairy-chested they are, compared with the man who's sitting next to them'.

Moya Dodd probably knows better than anyone the relationship between women, sport and power. Dodd is Australia's voice in global soccer: she's the vice-president of the Asian Football Confederation, deputy chairwoman of FIFA's Committee for Women's Football, one of the first women to serve on FIFA's executive committee and an FFA board member, and a former vice-captain of the Matildas to boot. Plus, in October 2016, she was named the overall winner of the 100 Women in Influence Awards for changing the global culture of football. Dodd says that a woman's role on boards isn't solely to benefit women:

The research will tell you that corruption flourishes in an environment that is homogenous and where group-think dominates. I absolutely do think that diversity, including gender diversity, is important in creating a better decision-making environment. One where the worst elements of sport governance can be reformed.

Dodd's own actions back this up. She was reportedly one of three FIFA executives to return a $25,000 Parmigiani watch given to each of them by Brazil's soccer body at the 2014 World Cup finals – an action later demanded of all executives by the FIFA Ethics Committee.

Claire Braund agrees that women have the power to change attitudes and reform old practices: 'Fans want to feel aligned with a sport's philosophy. They want more than a winning team. They want something that speaks to a culture of a better society. Poor behaviour could be averted by a strong female voice.' This isn't to say that all women act as moral compasses and all men are wayward – gender equality at board level is about recognising a great untapped resource. It's about broadening the talent pool.

Only when this happens can we, with a straight face, have a conversation about merit. The concept of selecting on 'merit' is spurious at best. As Jennifer Whelan, Research Fellow at the Asia-Pacific Social Impact Leadership Centre of the Melbourne Business School, points out, the merit-based system 'discriminates' on the basis of how much *perceived* 'merit' a person has, and perceptions of merit are shaped and influenced by gender stereotypes:

We know from research that men and women are stereotypically perceived to differ on two dimensions – women are perceived as interpersonally warmer and less competent relative to men, and men are perceived as less interpersonally warm and more competent relative to women.

These perceptions form the basis of gender stereotypes and unconscious bias. Once activated, stereotypes and unconscious bias exert an irresistible influence on our decision-making, without our awareness. An emphasis on merit in decision-making simply activates the stereotype that men and women differ in their degree of competence or capability.

Put simply, society pushes the view that men make more natural leaders.

Whelan draws upon research into major US orchestras to prove her point. Today, a third of the New York Philharmonic's members are women, but throughout most of the 1950s and '60s, the orchestra was all male. The soaring number of women players in the Philharmonic and other leading American orchestras doesn't reflect their improved musicianship; rather, a good part of the credit goes to the use of 'blind' auditions – tryouts that disguise the identity of aspiring players (playing behind a curtain). Selectors had long insisted that the lack of women musicians wasn't gender discrimination per se, but simply that the preferred playing style just so happened to predominate among male musicians. Of course, the introduction of blind auditions has put that defence to rest. When you can't take gender into account, women have just as much 'merit' as men – at least when it comes to musicians.

Unless Mozart's Violin Concerto No. 3 becomes a prerequisite for all new board appointments in sport, we're not going to see blind selection procedures. What we can demand are targets to increase the number of women in positions of influence. Calls for quotas are often met with claims that they're anti-meritocratic, when it's the opposite: quotas help establish merit by recognising the (usually dismissed) ability of half the population. The only way to change the perception of what a leader looks and sounds like is to rewrite the script and get more women into positions of power.

In March 2013, the Australian Sports Commission (ASC) announced that boards of funded NSOs would be required to meet a target of 40 per cent female representation by 2015, as part of its new Mandatory Sports Governance Principles, to bring them into line with expectations for Commonwealth boards and publicly listed company boards.

The top seven sports that receive more than A$5 million in government funding each year risk losing up to 20 per cent of that funding if they don't comply. Of those seven, only Hockey Australia has so far met the target for women on its board. While Hockey Australia is the lone shining example, the national governing bodies for athletics, swimming, cycling, rowing, sailing and basketball are under pressure to reform or risk having their funding docked. From 2014 the number of sports subject to the mandatory principles increased from seven to fifteen, with sports such as triathlon, canoe and netball added.

I've comfortably reached the point where I support a 50 per cent gender quota. I agree wholeheartedly in 'the best person for the job', but historically it hasn't played out that way. Selecting on 'merit' is skewed in favour of men, and so progress has been slow.

I've been listening to Wendy McCarthy talk about quotas for decades. A businesswoman as well as company director and co-founder of the Women's Electoral Lobby in New South Wales, McCarthy began her professional life as a secondary school teacher; she taught continuously for six years in Sydney, London and Pittsburgh, USA. The obstacles she faced to stay a teacher when she became a mother led her to community activism, then management and finally to the boardroom. She doesn't dance around the issue of quotas: 'We need a big objective – 50:50 by 2020 – because we need goals and targets so there are no more excuses. It's not just about board roles; it's also about the landscape of our workplaces and our domestic arrangements.'

McCarthy's right: it's about more than getting a prized seat around the polished mahogany table. It's about getting the entire organisation or sport to take gender equality seriously, it's about giving women a voice, it's about reflecting women's experiences and putting policies in place to allow for greater work–life flexibility for everyone.

*

Netball is one sport that's doing something about greater work–life flexibility. Its new pay deal gives women more support and incentives to return to the game if they choose to start a family. In addition to the player payments, national league athletes are entitled to a groundbreaking parental care policy for players with young children; private health insurance contributions of up to $1500 per annum, per player; and 100 per cent income protection on all earnings for up to two years in the event of injury or pregnancy.

Australian netball captain Laura Geitz announced her pregnancy in September 2016. Sharing her news with her Queensland Firebird teammates, Geitz said:

> This will be my last game in the purple dress for a while. I've been offered the most amazing job opportunity for next year that I just can't turn down. You get to a point in your life where you realise that when some job opportunities come along, they are just too good to let go... So, next year, I am going to be... a mum.

The team burst into cheers.

As it has throughout Australian sporting history, netball is leading the way. This is what all elite sports played by women should be doing – and perhaps in this new competitive environment for women's sport, others will follow suit with similar policies. It's important for this conversation to get started so that women don't have to confront the painful choice of being an elite athlete or a mother – we know that with the right support, they can be both. Only when family-friendly policies become the norm across all sports played by women will the stigma of being a mother in elite sport disappear.

Support and solutions can also be found at the grassroots level. Melbourne's Bayside City Council has twenty-seven sporting pavilions, fifty sports clubs, 1300 teams and twenty thousand club members – and a very high rate of participation in physical activity (compared to rest of Victoria). Yet 80 per cent of these pavilions pre-date 1960, and 96 per cent of them don't have appropriate change facilities for women. In response to this glaring problem, the council introduced a community campaign – supported by the *Bayside Leader* newspaper, which ran its own similar campaign 'The Grass Ceiling' – to raise awareness about the substandard sporting facilities for women and girls in the area.

Mayor Felicity Frederico led the charge:

We are calling on the Federal and Victorian governments to acknowledge the importance of sport for girls. All levels of government need to increase investment to accelerate the upgrade of sporting facilities to create a level playing field for women and girls. Inaction by governments simply means another generation will miss out or continue to accept second best. It is not appropriate for women and girls to have to use male toilets or to share changeroom facilities with an opposition team because there is only one set of female changerooms. It is also not good enough that girls are playing in cramped environments.

Brighton Vampires Junior Football Club has the largest number of female footy players in the South Metro Junior Football League, with four teams in three age groups: under-12s, under-15s and under-18s. Club President Ian Jensen-Muir says that better facilities send a strong message that women and girls are welcome at the club:

We are a mixed footy club that has been playing with the use of just two changerooms, both built with male facilities like open showers and urinals ... once the upgrade is complete, we will have four changerooms that will be configured appropriately for females, with more toilets and better privacy.

These types of improved facilities helps our girls feel welcomed into the club, and feel like they have a place here.

Bayside only has seven netball courts – a shortage of courts means that nearly two hundred players have a bye each week, and many other games are timed shorter to ensure that everyone can play.

The neighbouring Port Phillip Council has also seen an explosion in the number of women and girls signing up to play netball, but it has only two outdoor netball facilities: neither with lights.

We already know that the lack of appropriate facilities is a barrier to girls and women participating in sport. The Victorian and SA governments' $10 million funds for women's change rooms, announced in 2015, are the biggest investments in women's sporting participation ever made by an Australian state government. This should be a priority for all governments.

*

It's important for all of us, but seeing as men still hold the most sway in sporting conversations, it's especially important for them to speak up about discrimination whenever they see it. Gender equality isn't just about women. To call it a 'women's issue', as though it belongs with period pain and bra-cup size, is wrong and insulting – it frees *everyone* from the shackles of socially constructed gender norms.

The renowned sociologist and gender professor Michael Kimmel articulates this issue very well. In his 2015 TED Talk, 'Why Gender Equality is Good for Everyone – Men Included', he finished by saying:

> So, what we found is something really important, that gender equality is in the interest of countries, of companies, and of men, and their children and their partners, that gender equality is not a zero-sum game. It's not a win-lose. It is a win-win for everyone. And what we also know is we cannot fully empower women and girls unless we engage boys and men. We know this. And my position is that men need the very things that women have identified that they need to live the lives they say they want to live in order to live the lives that we say we want to live.

In sport, the easy option for a white privileged man is to be complicit, to accept all the trappings that come his way and not get involved in any discussions that challenge the status quo – apart from keeping the power base in the same old hands, it might just land him a plum role in the media. The bottom line is that gender equality can't be reached without men making room for women. This doesn't mean that swarms of helicopters are going to fly into the city and hover over corporate buildings, dropping down ropes from which wild-eyed women in combat trousers are going to abseil and storm into office boardrooms, demanding the top job and the installation of heated bathroom seats and in-house pedicurists.

Rather than get worked up about affirmative action, which redresses years of imbalance, consider these words from Professor Kimmel: 'So let me be very clear: white men in Europe and the United States [*you can add Australia too!*] are the beneficiaries of the single greatest affirmative action program in the history of the world. It is called "the history of the world".'

That's why Former Sex Discrimination Commissioner Elizabeth Broderick created Male Champions of Change in 2010: men handpicked to stand alongside women in order to drive change, not only within their organisations but more broadly too. The first group of champions targeted some of Australia's most influential male CEOs and chairmen from the business world, including Qantas, ANZ, Telstra, Commonwealth Bank, KPMG, Goldman Sachs, along with Former Chief of Army Lieutenant General David Morrison.

In 2015, a similar group was set up, comprising thirteen CEOs from seven major sports: AFL, NRL, A-League, tennis, swimming, basketball, cricket and the ASC. The Elite Sport Male Champions of Change grew from a 2014 research paper (commissioned by the forward-thinking Richmond Football Club) entitled 'Gender Equity: What It Will Take to Be the Best'. Almost sixty women from across the AFL industry were interviewed, and the findings include:

Women (and diversity more broadly) have to be part of the fabric of the organisation from board level and throughout in order to make equity part of the organisational DNA, rather than what has been seen to date as 'strategic window dressing'.

A deficit approach, where gender equity and women are seen as an 'issue', a problem to fix, is limited; diversity needs to be viewed from a different perspective focused firmly on what the [sic] contribution, knowledge, skill and assets women can bring to the equation.

On the role of men as learners and leaders, many women lamented the fact that much of the impetus for change to date on gender equity in sport has been left to women:

Most women agreed that men should be engaged in a more structured, deliberate and strategic way so they really have the opportunity to understand what is needed. There was a strong impression from interviewees that work to date had not gone far enough to really change men's views on the value of diversity, and the consequence of this was a perception that the game's position on gender equity was not much more than lip-service.

It is important to highlight that women did not think that men sit around the boardroom table plotting how they can prevent women from reaching leadership positions. To the contrary, many stories were shared of 'terrific men in footy committed to gender equality' and 'men who feel strongly about this and are throwing their full force behind leadership for women'.

The belief that most men are well-meaning when they say 'women will get there eventually, they just need support', was expressed often but the frustration from people was palpable, with one female leader saying she felt like screaming 'NO THEY WON'T, have a look at the evidence!'

That's been my experience in sport too: things stay the same because people don't know how to deal with change. If this continues, it will take an eternity for women to be treated as equals.

Men across the spectrum of sport have the muscle (literally) to stimulate discussion about gender equality and drive lasting change. The template for this is already here: sport is filled with men like Nicky Winmar and Adam Goodes who have stared racism in the face and won, often at enormous personal cost. And a new wave of politically aware footballers from all major codes have been adding their voices to the campaign to end violence against women.

Australian rugby union player and Brumbies captain David Pocock uses his public profile to raise awareness about sexism, homophobia, domestic violence and environmental issues. Geelong's Jimmy Bartel – who grew up with an abusive, alcoholic father – made a pledge not to shave his face or cut his hair for the entire 2016 AFL season, in the hope that whenever people saw his increasingly wild appearance, they would be reminded of his 'Face Up to DV' campaign. The word 'champion' is loosely applied to men in sport – by calling for a new conversation about what it means to be a man, Pocock and Bartel are legitimate champions.

Similarly, former Sydney Swans player Luke Ablett and current AFL players Patrick Dangerfield, Marcus Bontempelli and Shaun Burgoyne are ambassadors for Our Watch's 'The Line' campaign, which encourages young people aged twelve to twenty to develop healthy and equal relationships, and to reject violence. The campaign's long-term goal is to prevent violence against women and children by addressing factors such as gender inequality, violence-supportive and sexist attitudes, and rigid gender roles and stereotypes.

It's smart to partner with footballers in order to get this message out there. Just by being footballers, these men make an impression on people. Boys, in particular, get to see that it's possible to be both physically and morally strong. By presenting a healthier vision of masculinity, one that says it's okay to call out behaviours that hurt and disrespect others, these players are changing the sporting landscape and society for the better.

Men everywhere must get involved and become self-appointed champions of change, and to call out everyday sexism when they see and hear it. It's time for a renewed commitment across the sport sector to find solutions to the layers of inequality that make up women's sport – from the lack of girls' toilets at suburban sporting clubs through to the male-dominated boardrooms of our richest sports. This needs to be an industry-wide approach.

Perhaps the best starting point for sport is to take a look at the nationwide campaign to stop violence against women – it has cut through all the bullshit and reached the core of the problem. In the most painful of circumstances, Rosie Batty mustered the courage to gently lead the nation in a conversation about domestic violence that was desperately overdue. In a world first, Australia now has a framework for a consistent and integrated national approach to prevent violence against women and children.

Our Watch has been one of the organisations leading the way, with its 'Change the Story' campaign: 'Australia has a choice. We can change the story that currently sees a woman murdered every week by a current or former partner. We can choose a future where women and their children live free from violence.' This is what it sounds like to not shirk from an issue but to be a champion of change. This is true leadership.

Just as anti-violence campaigners have done, the sporting community must have a mature conversation about what keeps women marginalised in sport. We must expose the link between casual sexism, which demeans, degrades and diminishes women, and the bigger picture of inequality. If we're going to make a real and lasting difference to the sporting landscape in this country, we must tackle the attitudes that give rise to sexism and discrimination on the field, in boardrooms where decisions are made, and in the media.

It's time that sport joined the dots, and it's time for sport to 'change the story'.

# EPILOGUE

The unmistakable smell of barbecued sausages and caramelised onions drifts across the Brunswick Street Oval and hangs in the air, along with the sideline commentary coming from the clusters of mums and dads who patrol the outskirts of the ground. I'm here to watch my friend's daughter Esther play. On the oval, the players occasionally hear sporadic clapping, words of encouragement and shouts of 'mark it!' over their teammates' voices and the umpire's whistle, but only occasionally. The ball has been bounced, and it's now all about the footy. Watching on, I can see the change in the players' faces; they're less carefree, as though a button has been pressed – everyone wears a mask of focus and is locked into game mode, where the only things that matter are on field.

Esther waits. Timing is everything in this game, and Esther knows it. Her eyes are fixed ahead, homed in on the action, watching the ball move from teammate to teammate. The opposition is pressing hard, but her team's training moves are paying off – slick hand passes and strong running off the ball are moving the Sherrin up the ground. 'Come on, come on,' she mutters under her breath as she reads the play. And she reads it well. It's one of Esther's many strengths. Centre-half-forward is her patch, and it's her job to own it. She shuffles, transferring her weight from one foot to the other. Her defender is close by.

Some grey clouds have moved in from the west, and a light drizzle has started to fall. Esther wrings her hands in preparation and strokes her palms across the back of her shorts. Her defender is even closer – she can hear her breathing; she gives her a bump for good measure. Esther waits. The good players know when to run: they have an instinct that lets them gain those extra couple of metres needed, but it's a fine line. If she goes too early, she'll be ignored and out of position.

*So hold on, read the play and ... not yet, not yet ... and, go! Go!*

An explosion of pace over the first five steps leaves her defender three paces behind, and Esther's been spotted, a textbook move. In comes the ball, spiralling down against the darkening skies, and *thump* – a single sound, clean, secure and straight into her arms, tight against her chest. Never in doubt.

Now Esther can hear the applause from all corners of the boundary. She can hear her mum and her older brother. And she can hear me – I can't help myself! I've come to watch her play, and it's impossible not to be swept up in it all.

Without fuss, Esther turns around and lines up for goal. On a slight angle, about fifteen metres out. Four deep breaths; she looks down at the ball, the familiar stitching; she spins it in her hands, then looks up at the goals once, twice. She's practised this kick a thousand times, like all the greats before her on this hallowed turf of the Brunswick Street Oval – Bunton Sr, Smallhorn, Ruthven, Moriarty and Murray. Autopilot kicks in, and in she runs, dropping the ball onto her right foot. As soon as it leaves Esther's boot, she knows, and she watches on as the ball sails through for another six points.

*We will always fight for victory, and we will always see it through.*

Home to the VFL Fitzroy Football Club from 1897 to 1966, the Brunswick Street Oval has seen many incarnations of the home team – from the Maroons to the Gorillas to the Lions to the Red Roys. The nicknames may have changed, but the spirit has not – at the ground, it's impossible not to feel it. That why I'm drawn to this place, that's why I'm here at the game, so I can see it close up and let it wash over me.

The spirit of the Brunswick Street Oval lives on through its people and stories. Many of the parents and grandparents watching on get a glaze of nostalgia in their eyes when they tell me their footy stories: 'I was here, Round 10, 1963 when …' As the story goes, Kevin Murray and Graham Campbell were unavailable due to interstate selection, and a number of other key players were out injured. No one gave the Lions any hope of winning. The selectors rolled the dice and made eight changes that Thursday evening; seven of the inclusions were teenagers. Fourteen players in the Fitzroy side had played less than twenty VFL senior games. Against the odds, Fitzroy defeated the star-studded Geelong Cats by 38-points. It was 'one of the most remarkable victories in Fitzroy's history'.

This is a club and ground full of history and full of stories – and now Esther is part of its story. Esther is an Under 12s Roy Girl.

*We are the girls from old Fitzroy,*
*We wear the colours maroon and blue.*
*We will always fight for victory,*

*We will always see it through.*
*Win or lose, we do or die,*
*In defeat we always try.*
*Fitzroy.*
*Fitzroy.*
*The club we hold so dear,*
*Premiers we'll be this year.*

When Esther speaks to me about her love of footy, like a lot of young people with a love, she talks passionately. She also talks clearly. And she sees things very clearly. It doesn't make sense to Esther to compete against boys; she doesn't want to play footy with boys. Why would she? She's a girl – a capable, talented, feisty girl who loves to compete against her own kind, and there are plenty of them. They play footy, talk footy, watch footy, argue about footy, sleep, eat and breathe footy. Some have brothers; some don't. Some have fathers who are interested in footy; some don't. Some have mothers who kick the ball with them; some don't. They all come from a wide range of backgrounds with a wide range of influences, but the one common thread is footy. Esther tells me that all her friends who love the game feel the same way – and she has a lot of friends who love the game. Girls' footy is the fastest-growing segment of the game. Esther and her friends don't make a big deal of it; they may not even know they're busting gender stereotypes and creating change, but that's exactly what they're doing. The revolution is coming, and Esther is part of it.

*

Standing here on the grass with history changing before my eyes makes me more sure than ever that the word 'woman' has to stay in sport. Esther and her friends in an all-girls' team have only just arrived. Women in the AFL, women in the Big Bash League, women in rugby sevens: they've only just arrived on the big stage. The only way for these sports to grow and become fully entrenched in the Australian sporting psyche is for the word 'woman' to be celebrated, not hidden. Let's get it up in lights – big, bold, brash (and beautiful) for all to see.

First things first: we need to let the word 'woman' bed itself in, we need to give it a chance to breathe in its own right, we need people to get used to it, so it's not such a big deal. We know that in order for this to happen, we've got a fair bit of catching up to do. We've joined the party late – in some cases centuries after men – and this means that we can't just swan in and expect lift-off. Just because I rock up to the King Island coastline decked out in a one-piece, a tub of grease and a smile doesn't mean that I can swim Bass Strait and look forward to a glass of bubbly on the shores of Apollo Bay; I need to have put in meticulous planning and preparation (along with some specially designed jet-propelled flippers and a submarine). We have to know who we are, our strengths and weaknesses, and we can't do that by taking the word 'woman' out of the equation.

In a better world, there would be no distinctions needed between sportspeople. For that to happen, though, women must be firmly embedded in the landscape – and embedded on their terms. We know this isn't a perfect world; however, we can feel very optimistic that we're moving in the right direction, and the discussion about taking the word 'woman' out of sport shouldn't detract from that – the fact that anyone can even think like that is a massive leap forward.

But what we don't want to see is women melded with men like some embarrassing appendage. We don't want to be desperately hanging from their coattails, mumbling through gritted teeth, 'What about me?!' We know from the long history of women's sports being underfunded, undervalued and actively discouraged that trying to blend in without much fuss isn't the answer. Women need to make noise. Women need to disrupt business as usual. Women need tournaments that stand alone and our own sustainable leagues. Girls need role models, who in turn need support from everybody so that they can get to the top.

Women need to be celebrated in their own right. And right now is the time to celebrate the word 'woman' in sport – in any sport. So let's stop undervaluing the strengths and skills that are more common among women than men. Let's embrace our differences.

Over the past twenty years, I've seen slow change (like watching three-toed sloths take on the Marathon des Sables). I've seen more girls and women playing sports traditionally played by boys and men, and more women in the sports media, and there are more women in administration and on sporting boards. But the most exciting changes have been in the past two years. At last the conversation is shifting from a 'what to do about women' debate to a debate about the cost of *not* including female talent if the sport wants to remain competitive in a dynamic, fast-paced entertainment industry. More importantly, sports are talking about including women as a moral issue, a matter of equality. Girls should be given the same opportunities and access to resources as boys. Women should be able to compete as professionals. Equality should be a pillar of a decent and progressive society.

I'd been thinking about writing this book for a long time. When I finally got around to it in 2015, I knew that things were changing, I knew there had been a subtle shift in the national consciousness – reports on the news, articles in newspapers, feedback from friends, from people involved in sport at all levels, from grassroots right up to the top – all this told me that something was in the air. What I could never have imagined was the pace at which it has taken hold. The speed at which things have snowballed has been the part that's amazed me most. And the sports themselves have lifted their game – in the new competitive environment, AFL, netball, cricket and soccer are pushing each other to be better and fairer.

Not so long ago, if you criticised the sporting landscape, stirred the pot or agitated for change in sport, you were dismissed as radical. But recently it's become more acceptable to take a stand for equality – now not a day goes by without a positive story in the mainstream media about women in sport. I can't keep up! It's a wonderful, wonderful feeling – we know how much can be achieved when everyone gets behind an idea. When everyone embraces a way of thinking and people see change, it becomes infectious and causes more change. When people see what equality in sport looks like and that it makes not just economic sense but also moral sense, there's a gathering of momentum towards making sport a better place – and what's happening right now makes me, for the first time ever, believe this is achievable.

\*

Esther reminds me of my eleven-year-old self. Watching her at the Brunswick Street Oval gave me goosebumps. And hope. The sight of her running free and hard, surrounded by girls all driven by the same desire to play the game and be as good as they can be, shows how far we've come. I remembered how I felt about netball, how much I obsessed over it. I can still remember the time, vividly, when I was eleven and believed that I could be the best centre-court player known to humankind – faster, fitter and trickier than the rest of the competition. Thinking of this takes me back to my childhood, to the clothesline and the square patch of lawn where my brother and I, armed only with a tennis ball, practised our catches for hours and hours into the fading light.

The difference between eleven-year-old Esther and eleven-year-old me is the path ahead. No one can curtail Esther – her world is bursting with possibilities. Stop signs don't exist there.

Esther can aspire to become a professional AFL player. She can one day represent her beloved Carlton in the women's league. To guide her, she'll have strong, visible role models in the game; she'll watch them on game day, see them on television, hear them on radio, read their stories and perhaps even collect their faces on footy swap cards. She'll see them get drafted, she'll see them debut, kick their first AFL goal, take mark of the year, rupture an ACL, get another sleeve tattoo over the summer, win the competition's best and fairest, run out on Grand Final day and hold the Premiership Cup aloft.

In Esther's world, those desperately clinging to gender stereotypes will be a small voice. Esther won't have to continually justify her decision to play Australian Rules football or defend tired, anachronistic claims that women's sport is rubbish and boring. She won't have to sit and wait for someone to call out a sexist comment or joke, because she'll be in the majority. The dark underbelly of sexism, along with racism and homophobia, will be exposed for the pitiful thing that it is. If Esther wants to promote her body first, it will be her choice and her choice alone – it won't be forced upon her by her sport, sponsors and the media. Esther will be the one in control of her destiny, the one pulling the strings.

Comedian Sarah Silverman captures the sentiment of Esther's world perfectly: 'Stop telling girls they can be anything they want when they grow up. I think it's a mistake. Not because they can't, but because it would never have occurred to them that they couldn't.'

In Esther's world, it won't be unusual for girls to play Australian Rules, soccer, rugby, rugby league or cricket. Girls will be encouraged to be who they want to be, and to run, fight and throw like a girl. It will be okay to be a girl – any kind of girl. Most men will be stronger, run faster and leap higher, but sport will be fairer. Perhaps, eventually, we'll even be able to take the word 'woman' out of it, because the playing field will at last be equal. Hopefully in Esther's world, traits such as strength, assertiveness and independence will be valued equally. Being a girl who plays sport will be okay. Actually, it will be better than okay – it will be fantastic.

And so will being a woman in sport.

# REFERENCES

*All websites accessed November 2016*

## 2. This Is a Man's World

**Page 27**: 'Although social attitudes toward participation ...'
Richards, Ralph (ed), 'Women's Sport', Clearinghouse
for Sport, the Australian Sports Commission, accessed
November 2016 https://www.clearinghouseforsport.gov.au/
knowledge_base/organised_sport/sport_and_government_
policy_objectives/womens_sport

**Page 29**: 'At a Special General Meeting held for members at
Lord's ...' and 'If we were debating tonight whether to have
fruit machines in the Long Room ...' Duncan, Isabelle,
*Skirting the Boundary: A History of Women's Cricket*, The
Robson Press, 2013

**Page 30**: 'At the age of twelve, one is unaware of the problems
ahead ...' Cooke, Nicole, 'Nicole Cooke's retirement
statement in full', the *Guardian*, 15 January 2013 https://
www.theguardian.com/sport/2013/jan/14/nicole-cooke-
retirement-statement

**Page 38:** 'I just wonder if her dad ...' 'John Inverdale "has written to Marion Bartoli over remark"', BBC News, 7 July 2013 http://www.bbc.com/news/uk-23214821

### 3. The Chicken and the Egg

**Page 44:** 'Indecency, ugliness, and impropriety were strong reasons ...' Leigh, Mary, 'Pierre de Coubertin: A man of his time', *Quest*, Volume 22, Issue 1, 1974, pp.19–24

**Page 45:** 'television coverage of women's sport had declined markedly ...' Lumby, Catharine, Capie, Helen and Greenwood, Kate, 'Towards a Level Playing Field: sport and gender in Australian media', Clearinghouse for Sport, the Australian Sports Commission, January 2008–July 2009, last updated January 2014 https://www.clearinghouseforsport.gov.au/__data/assets/pdf_file/0010/595567/Towards_a_level_playing_field_-_Updated_Version.pdf

**Page 46:** 'A more recent Australian Sports Commission (ASC) report ...' Paterson, James and Matzelle, Ryan for Repucom, 'Women in Sport Broadcasting Analysis: Final Report', Clearinghouse for Sport, the Australian Sports Commission, April 2014 https://www.clearinghouseforsport.gov.au/__data/assets/pdf_file/0007/615913/Women_in_Sport_Broadcasting_Analysis_April_2012_-_March_2014.PDF

**Page 47:** 'Dr Litchfield and her CSU colleague Dr Jaquelyn Osborne conducted their own research into newspaper coverage of gendered sports ...' Litchfield, Chelsea and

Osborne, Jaquelyn, 'Women in the Sports Pages: A Brief Insight into Olympic and Non-Olympic Years in Australia', *The International Journal of Sport and Society*, Volume 4, Issue 4, February 2015, pp.45–56

**Page 48:** 'In the latest Australian Bureau of Statistics study …' 'Participation in Sport and Physical Recreation, Australia, 2013–14', the Australian Bureau of Statistics, 2015 http://www.abs.gov.au/ausstats/abs@.nsf/mf/4177.0

'Interestingly, the ASC's "Women in Sport Broadcasting" …' Paterson, James and Matzelle, Ryan for Repucom, 'Women in Sport Broadcasting Analysis: Final Report', Clearinghouse for Sport, the Australian Sports Commission April, 2014 https://www.clearinghouseforsport.gov. au/__data/assets/pdf_file/0007/615913/Women_in_Sport_ Broadcasting_Analysis_April_2012_-_March_2014.PDF

**Page 49:** 'Men's sports are going to seem more exciting …' Cooky, Cheryl, Messner, Michael and Mustto, Michela, '"It's Dude Time!": A Quarter Century of Excluding Women's Sports in Televised News and Highlight Shows', *Communication & Sport*, Volume 3, Number 3, September 2015, pp.261–287 http://com.sagepub.com/ content/3/3/261.full.pdf+html

**Page 55:** 'Russell Jackson's piece in the *Guardian* during the Chris Gayle controversy …' Jackson, Russel, 'It's not just Chris Gayle: sport media's Blokesworld mindset needs to change', the *Guardian*, 5 January 2016 https://www. theguardian.com/sport/blog/2016/jan/05/its-not-just-chris-gayle-sport-medias-blokesworld-mindset-needs-to-change

**Page 58:** 'media distribution will be highly tailored to the customers' wants and needs ...' Lumby, Catharine, Capie, Helen and Greenwood, Kate, 'Towards a Level Playing Field: sport and gender in Australian media', Clearinghouse for Sport, the Australian Sports Commission, January 2008 – July 2009, last updated January 2014 https://www.clearinghouseforsport.gov.au/__data/assets/pdf_file/0010/595567/Towards_a_level_playing_field_-_Updated_Version.pdf

**Page 60:** 'A key recommendation of the ASC report ...' Lumby, Catharine, Capie, Helen and Greenwood, Kate, 'Towards a Level Playing Field: sport and gender in Australian media', Clearinghouse for Sport, the Australian Sports Commission, January 2008 – July 2009, last updated January 2014 https://www.clearinghouseforsport.gov.au/__data/assets/pdf_file/0010/595567/Towards_a_level_playing_field_-_Updated_Version.pdf

**Page 61:** 'RMIT University (2015) found that women are twice as likely to be targeted ...' Ryan, Kelly, 'Online abuse affects 3 in 5 Australians: study', RMIT University News, 16 November 2015 http://www.rmit.edu.au/news/all-news/2015/november/online-abuse-affects-3-in-5-australians-study

## 4. The Beauty Game

**Page 64:** 'In 2015, for the sixth year in a row, Mission Australia's National Youth Survey identified body image ...' Cave, L., Fildes, J., Luckett, G. and Wearring, A., 'Mission Australia's 2015 Youth Survey Report', Mission Australia, 2015

'Further highlighting these issues is the "Everyday Sexism" report ...' 'Everyday Sexism: Girls' and young women's views on gender inequality in Australia', *Our Watch*, October 2016

**Page 66:** 'The public image of female athletes is defined to a large degree by the media ...' Hargreaves, Jennifer, *Heroines of Sport: The Politics of Difference and Identity*, Psychology Press, 2000

**Page 68:** 'Although the renewal of French sport was expected following the Liberation ...' Attali, Michael and Saint-Martin, Jean, 'A View of the 1948 Olympics from Across the Channel: An Analysis of the French Press', *The International Journal of the History of Sport*, Volume 27, Number 6, 2010, pp.1047–1064

**Page 76:** 'eight of the world's top ten highest-paid female athletes of 2016 were tennis players ...' 'The World's Highest-Paid Female Athletes 2016', *Forbes*, June 2016 http://www.forbes.com/pictures/mli45ffmff/the-worlds-highest-paid/#12590c29729c

**Page 78:** 'Flick through Leisel Jones's 2015 memoir, *Body Lengths* ...' Jones, Leisel and McLean, Felicity, *Body Lengths*, Nero, 2015

**Page 82:** 'When you look at how men are portrayed and women are portrayed ...' Turnbull, Samantha and Shoebridge, Joanne, 'Researcher says women surfers under-paid and over-sexualised', ABC News, June 2015.

## 5. Invisibility

**Page 91:** 'Wilson was named in the *2014 Wisden Cricketers' Almanack* as one of its five greatest female cricketers of all time ...' Booth, Lawrence, *2014 Wisden Cricketers' Almanack*, Wisden, June 2014

## 6. Garnish

**Page 98:** '(It) boasts the highest percentage of bare flesh per driver ...' Turner, Beverly, *The Pits: The Real World of Formula One*, Atlantic Books, 2005

**Page 99:** 'A letter from F1 chief Bernie Ecclestone in May 2013 ...' Kent, David, 'Bernie Ecclestone reveals Formula One grid passes should be given to "celebrities or really glamorous ladies" in leaked letter sent to former team principal of Caterham', the *Daily Mail*, 5 March 2015 http://www.dailymail.co.uk/sport/formulaone/article-2979770/Bernie-Ecclestone-reveals-Formula-One-grid-passes-given-celebrities-really-glamorous-ladies.html

**Page 100:** 'A 2015 survey of over three thousand young men and women commissioned by Our Watch ...' Hall & Partners Open Mind, 'The Line campaign: summary of research findings', *Our Watch*, 2015 http://www.ourwatch.org.au/MediaLibraries/OurWatch/our-publications/The-Line-campaign-Research-summary-AA-28-May-2015_1.docx

**Page 105:** 'Or, as the Bettingpro website puts it in a 2014 post ...' 'Premier League Darts Walk On Girls – Our Top 7 Darts Babes', Bettingpro, 16 October 2014 http://www.

bettingpro.com/category/darts/premier-league-darts-walk-on-girls-our-top-7-darts-babes-201402130041/

## 7. The Wage Gap

'Australia's Latest Gender Equality Scorecard', the Workplace Gender Equality Agency for the Australian Government https://www.wgea.gov.au/sites/default/files/2014-15-WGEA_SCORECARD.pdf

Page 115: 'There is a lot of discrimination against mothers …' Bossi, Dominic, 'Women's World Cup 2015: Matildas goalkeeper Melissa Barbieri learning from group rivals USA', 7 June 2015 http://www.smh.com.au/sport/soccer/womens-world-cup-2015-matildas-goalkeeper-melissa-barbieri-learning-from-group-rivals-usa-20150607-ghiij0.html

## 8. The Dark Underbelly

Page 123: 'You know, it may raise things that have been long forgotten …' Transcript of Fullerton, Ticky, 'Fair Game', *Four Corners*, Australian Broadcasting Corporation. Sourced from Clearinghouse for Sport, the Australian Sport Commission, May 2004 https://www.clearinghouseforsport.gov.au/__data/assets/pdf_file/0003/557040/Fair_game_-_Four_corners_transcript_ABC.pdf

Page 125: 'In 2009, seven North Melbourne players produced a video called "The Adventures of Little Boris" …' Lane, Samantha, 'North Melbourne in damage control after player posts misogynistic chicken video online', the *Age*, 8

April 2009 http://www.theage.com.au/news/rfnews/north-in-damage-control/2009/04/07/1238869972286.html

'Here's how the *Herald Sun*'s Superfooty reported it …' 'Boris the rubber chicken breaks silence over chook-sex', Superfooty, the *Herald Sun*, sourced from PerthNow.com. au http://www.perthnow.com.au/news/boris-breaks-silence-over-video/story-e6frg12c-1225698817322

Page 128: 'Two former detectives claimed that colleagues …' McMahon, Stephen and Hunt, Elissa, 'Police admit that former cop who alleges Stephen Milne rape charge case collapsed amid threats made complaint years ago', the *Herald Sun*, 22 June 2010 http://www.heraldsun.com. au/news/st-kilda-players-in-shock-sex-cover-up-claim/story-e6frf7jo-1225882432318 and Hunt, Elissa, 'Claims of police corruption in Stephen Milne case from 2004', the *Herald Sun*, 21 June 2010 http://www.foxsports.com. au/afl/claims-of-police-corruption-in-stephen-milne-case-from-2004/story-e6frf3e3-1225921758788

'In 2012, the Office of Police Interity called for a review …' Moor, Keith, 'Stephen Milne "rape" investigation sufficient – OPI', the *Herald Sun*, 30 May 2012 http://www. heraldsun.com.au/news/stephen-milne-rape-investigation-sufficient-opi/story-e6frf7jo-1226374062701

'… the sex crime squad decided that it had enough evidence to charge Milne … Victoria Police released a statement conceding that the original investigation was "substantially inadequate" …' Oakes, Dan, 'Nine years late an investigation drops a bombshell', the *Age*, 19 June 2013 http://www.theage.com.au/afl/afl-news/nine-years-later-an-investigation-drops-a-bombshell-20130618-2ogwl.html

'At the committal hearing in the Melbourne Magistrates Court ...' Baxendale, Rachel, 'Committal hearing told Milne persisted with sex despite objections', the *Australian*, 12 November 2013 http://www.theaustralian.com.au/news/nation/committal-hearing-told-milne-persisted-with-sex-despite-objections/story-e6frg6nf-1226758150556

**Page 129:** 'Montagna said he'd heard the woman say "no" ...' Cooper, Adam, 'Nobody was forced to have sex: Montagna', the *Age*, 13 November 2013 http://www.theage.com.au/victoria/nobody-was-forced-to-have-sex-montagna-20131113-2xfyk.html

'Milne was to face trial for rape charges in 2014, but the charges were discontinued ...' Flower, Wayne, Deery, Shannon and Portelli, Emily, 'Stephen Milne, former St Kilda player pleads guilty to indecent assault as rape charges are dropped', the *Herald Sun*, 6 November 2014 http://www.heraldsun.com.au/news/law-order/stephen-milne-former-st-kilda-player-pleads-guilty-to-indecent-assault-as-rape-charges-are-dropped/news-story/1532a089f904caa1251ee739ec687bfc

'... was fined $15,000 ...' Flower, Wayne, 'Stephen Milne avoids conviction for assaulting woman; rape case was dropped', the *Age*, 18 November 2014 http://www.heraldsun.com.au/news/law-order/stephen-milne-avoids-conviction-for-assaulting-woman-rape-case-was-dropped/news-story/b57141dd4f0ec05d0e333470dd0d3c0e

**Page 130:** 'the Red Cliff Tigers said that they were "extremely excited to have Nick on board ..."' Driscoll, Hannah, 'Nick Stevens announced as new senior coach for Red Cliffs', the *Weekly Times*, 26 November 2015 http://www. weeklytimesnow.com.au/sport/country-football/nick-stevens-announced-as-new-senior-coach-for-red-cliffs/news-story/89996dc9b1fece97acd3947755ba2cae

'AFL Victoria intervened to stop him coaching the Tigers ...' Doherty, Elissa, 'AFL intervenes as convicted former AFL star Nick Stevens appointed coach of local side ahead of court appeal', the *Herald Sun*, 2 December 2015 http:// www.heraldsun.com.au/news/victoria/convicted-former-afl-star-nick-stevens-has-been-appointed-senior-coach-of-a-local-side-despite-a-pending-court-appeal/news-story/0e912 ff27611d804d413220832df206e

'In July 2016, he was jailed for three months and fined $3000 ...' Iaria, Melissa, 'Ex-AFL player Nick Stevens jailed for three months for assault on ex-girlfriend', the *Age*, 21 July 2016 http://www.theage.com.au/afl/afl-news/former-afl-player-nick-stevens-admits-injuring-expartner-20160721-gqahi6.html

'In 2011, West Coast's Patrick McGinnity sledged ...' Lane, Samantha, 'Eagle suspended over "rape sledge" the *Age*, 17 August 2011 http://www.theage.com.au/afl/afl-news/eagle-suspended-over-rape-sledge-20110816-1iwgf.html

## 9. Complicity

**Page 137:** 'The fact is that men encounter more complicity in their woman ...' de Beauvoir, Simone, *The Second Sex*, Random House, April 2010. (First published in 1949)

**Page 138:** 'Former Victorian Police commissioner Ken Lay cried when he read, in a survey of community attitudes towards family violence ...' 'Family violence advisory chair Ken Lay "brought to tears" by childrens' attitudes', ABC News, 25 November 2015 http://www.abc.net.au/news/2015-11-25/ken-lay-brought-to-tears-by-domestic-violence-stories/6971894

**Page 140:** 'In 2014, Wallabies utility back Kurtley Beale sent two lewd messages containing pictures of obese women ...' Payten, Iain, 'Kurtley Beale's exchange with Di Patston – Wallabies star pleaded for forgiveness over crude text messages', the *Courier Mail*, October 2014 http://www.couriermail.com.au/sport/rugby/kurtley-beales-exchange-with-di-patston-wallabies-star-pleaded-for-forgiveness-over-crude-text-messages/news-story/549f2b48cd26d36baaa07e04030cd1a4

'There's that kind of double bind ...' Hayes, Martha, 'Hillary Clinton's best quotes: Women's rights are human rights', *Marie Claire*, 15 November 2016 http://www.marieclaire.co.uk/entertainment/people/hillary-clinton-quotes-to-make-you-feel-truly-empowered-42730#33xuV6lcvqvybOxE.99

**Page 142:** 'This is what happens when women name what's happening ...' Transcript of Leigh Sales interview with Penny Wong, 'Penny Wong reflects on Slipper storm and political climate', *7.30*, ABC News, October 2012 http://

www.abc.net.au/7.30/content/2012/s3608049.htm

**Page 143:** 'In the lead-up to the London Olympics, Australian swimmers …' Jeffrey, Nicole, 'Stilnox scandal fallout deepens as James Magnussen breaks ranks', the *Australian*, 25 February 2013 http://www.theaustralian. com.au/sport/stilnox-scandal-fallout-deepens/story-e6frg7mf-1226584584249

## 10. Game Changers

**Page 152:** 'there was some public discussion about Mayweather's shocking history of domestic violence …' Yuhas, Alan, 'Floyd Mayweather's domestic violence history clouds fight as female reporters say they were banned', the *Guardian*, 3 May 2015 https://www. theguardian.com/sport/2015/may/02/floyd-mayweather-cnn-espn-reporters-say-banned-fight

**Page 155:** 'Her post-ride interview was as game-changing as her brilliant ride …' Decent, Tom, 'Melbourne Cup 2015: Winning jockey Michelle Payne hits back at doubters after making history on Prince of Penzance', the *Sydney Morning Herald*, 3 November 2015 http://www.smh.com.au/sport/horseracing/melbourne-cup-2015-winning-jockey-michelle-payne-hits-back-at-doubters-after-making-history-on-prince-of-penzance-20151103-gkpouv.html

**Page 158:** 'One South Australian Member of Parliament described suffragists as …' Haines, Janine, 'Suffrage to Sufferance: 100 Years of Women in Parliament', *Papers on Parliament*, No. 17, September

1992 http://www.aph.gov.au/~/~/link.aspx?_
id=780C87B08CF94FD8908FE0CC62EB3513&_z=z

### 13. A League of Her Own

**Page 206:** 'the woman decided not to make a statement to
police and they eventually dropped their investigation ...'
Buttler, Mark and Landsberger, Sam, 'No police action
against Richmond's Dustin Martin over altercation with
woman', the *Herald Sun*, 22 December 2015 http://www.
heraldsun.com.au/news/police-will-not-take-action-against-
richmonds-dustin-martin-over-threats-against-woman/news-
story/0bd9906c04ffd8e60721016415f5fdf2

'the AFL also cleared Martin of any serious wrongdoing
but Richmond slapped him with a $5000 suspended fine
...' Murnane, Matt, 'Dustin Martin cleared of serious
misconduct, given suspended fine by Richmond', the
*Age*, 14 January 2016 http://www.theage.com.au/afl/afl-
news/dustin-martin-cleared-of-serious-misconduct-given-
suspended-fine-by-richmond-20160114-gm5slp.html

### 14. The Price of Equality

**Page 211:** 'In the past four weeks the Matildas have been
mentioned over five hundred ...' Tulloch, Brihony, 'Media
waltz right past Matildas, showering loser Socceroos with
love', 30 June 2015 https://www.crikey.com.au/2015/06/30/
media-waltz-right-past-matildas-showering-loser-socceroos-
with-love/

**Page 222:** 'One of our key strategies as a board and as a CEO

...' Doutre, Tim, 'Men, women and hockey's level paying field', the *New Daily*, 27 July 2015 http://thenewdaily.com.au/sport/hockey/2015/07/27/men-women-hockeys-level-playing-field

### 15. Making Ourselves Heard

**Page 236:** 'Dodd says that a woman's role on boards isn't solely to benefit women ...' Timna, Jacks, 'Australia's top sportswomen still stuck in the shadows', the *Sydney Morning Herald*, 31 January 2015 http://www.smh.com.au/sport/australias-top-sportswomen-still-stuck-in-the-shadows-20141220-12be8g.html **Page 237:** 'the merit-based system "discriminates" on the basis of how much perceived 'merit' a person has ...' Whelan, Jennifer, 'The myth of merit and unconscious bias', the Conversation, 16 October 2013 http://theconversation.com/the-myth-of-merit-and-unconscious-bias-18876

**Page 237:** 'the merit-based system "discriminates" on the basis of how much perceived "merit" a person has ...' Whelan, Jennifer, 'The myth of merit and unconscious bias', the Conversation, 16 October 2013 http://theconversation.com/the-myth-of-merit-and-unconscious-bias-18876

**Page 239:** 'In March 2013, the Australian Sports Commission announced that ...' Lane, Samantha, 'Sports dragging the chain on women-on-boards target', the *Sydney Morning Herald,* 10 May 2015 http://www.smh.com.au/sport/sports-dragging-the-chain-on-womenonboards-target-20150510-ggy8kk.html

**Page 240:** 'We need a big objective – 50:50 by 2020 …' Quoted in Porter, Jeni, 'Wendy McCarthy, Karen Wilson, Diane Grady, Ita Buttrose, Helen Lynch and others on women's progress', the *Australian*, 3 December 2015 http://www.theaustralian.com.au/business/the-deal-magazine/wendy-mccarthy-karen-wilson-diane-grady-ita-buttrose-helen-lynch-and-others-on-womens-progress/news-story/339a11a70e8a3cc98656341f5b6b0033

**Page 241:** 'This will be my last game in the purple dress for a while …' Houle, Alexandra, 'Firebirds captain Laura Geitz has announced she is expecting her first child', Mamamia, 11 September 2016 http://www.mamamia.com.au/laura-geitz-is-expecting/

**Page 242:** 'We are calling on the Federal and Victorian governments to acknowledge the importance of sport for girls …' 'Doing it for the Girls', *CiVic Magazine*, Winter 2016. https://issuu.com/civic-magazine/docs/civic_winter_2016

**Page 245:** 'The Elite Sport Male Champions of Change grew from a 2014 research paper …' 'Gender Equity: What it will take to be the best', the Richmond Football Club in partnership with Blueston Edge, the Australian Football League and the Australian Sports Commission, July 2014 http://s.afl.com.au/staticfile/AFL%20Tenant/Richmond/Files/Gender%20Report.pdf

## Epilogue

**Page 253:** 'one of the most remarkable …' Spaull, Roger,

'Bryan Clements – Fitzroy FC – a day to remember at the Brunswick Oval', Boyles Football Photos, 18 May 2014 http://www.boylesfootballphotos.net.au/article55-Bryan-Clements-Fitzroy-FC-A-Day-To-Remember-At-The-Brunswick-Street-Oval

# ACKNOWLEDGEMENTS

A big thank you goes to Martin Hughes at Affirm Press for taking on the book and believing so wholeheartedly in the importance of its subject matter.

To my editor, Ruby Ashby-Orr, thank you for being my champion cornerwoman throughout this whole process, and thank you for helping me shape the themes and focus of the book – and for your wonderful spirit. I'd like to pass on those same sentiments to Kate Goldsworthy, who brilliantly finetuned it and put all the jigsaw pieces together (and thank you Jo Case for casting your laser eye over the final polish).

To my literary agent, and friend, Jacinta Di Mase, thanks for backing me (and having my back), and thanks for making things happen in the best kind of way.

And to all the women in sport – the athletes, the administrators, my colleagues in the media and all the fans, thank you for inspiring me to keep up the fight. And, of course, I mustn't forget the army of girls whose love of sport and indomitable spirit continue to inspire me and make all this worthwhile.

I've saved the most important thank yous till last. Thank you Francis for being everything I ever wanted and more, and thank you Simon, my love, for your help and guidance throughout this process – I couldn't have done it without you.